Sermons on the
Spiritual Life

Copyright © 2020 by Patristic Nectar Publications
ALL RIGHTS RESERVED
Printed in the USA

Illustrations by Predrag Ilievski. Drawings by Vladimir and Goce Ilievski.
All interior illustrations and artwork, Copyright © Newrome Press.

Publisher's Cataloging-In-Publication Data

Names: Filaret, Metropolitan of Moscow, 1782-1867, author. | Ilievski, Predrag, illustrator. | Kotar, Nicholas, translator.

Title: Sermons on the spiritual life / Saint Philaret of Moscow ; illustrations by Predrag Ilievski ; [translated by Deacon Nicholas Kotar].

Other Titles: Sermons. Selections. English

Description: [Riverside, California] : Patristic Nectar Publications, [2020]

Identifiers: ISBN 9781735011608

Subjects: LCSH: Russkai︠a︡ pravoslavnai︠a︡ t︠s︡erkov'--Sermons. | Spiritual life. | Sermons, Russian.

Classification: LCC BX513 .F55 2020 | DDC 252.019--dc23

SAINT PHILARET OF MOSCOW

Sermons *on the* Spiritual Life

SAINT PHILARET OF MOSCOW

Contents

Foreword vii

Introduction ix

1. On Being Born Again 1
2. On Gratitude to God 9
3. On the Fear of God 17
4. On Pious Zeal 23
5. On Poverty of Spirit 30
6. On the Purification of the Heart 36
7. On Consecrating the Day of the Lord 41
8. On Blessed Childbearing 48
9. On Love of Work 55
10. On Works of Mercy 62
11. On the Faith of those Who Seek to Touch Jesus 70
12. On Cheesefare Sunday. Against Intemperance. 76
13. On the Proper Preparation for Prayer 83
14. On the Lord's Prayer 91
15. On Praying with the Spirit and Understanding 101
16. On the Rest of Those Who Labor and are Heavy Laden 109
17. On the Easy Yoke of Christ 117
18. On the Parable of the Tares 124
19. On Stumbling Blocks 131
20. On Heavenly Rewards 137
21. On Our Citizenship in Heaven 143

Foreword

It is with great joy that Patristic Nectar Publications offers this volume of St. Philaret of Moscow's homilies entitled Sermons on the Spiritual Life. For decades divine energy proceeded forth from the mouth of St. Philaret as his sermons transformed the lives of countless individuals, and established the Saint's reputation as the Russian Chrysostom. In the 19th century spiritually thirsty men and women traveled from great distances throughout the world to Moscow to hear the Word of God from the Saint's lips. The Complete Sermons of St. Philaret in multiple volumes have nourished Slavic believers for the last 150 years, but English speakers have been almost completely deprived of his God-inspired teachings. We at PNP hope that this English-language volume will be followed by additional English-language translations of the Saint's sermons in the near future. In this day of homiletical mediocrity the reader can find in these homilies the life-giving words of one who embraced the asceticism of preaching to the salvation of countless souls.

Father Josiah Trenham
Patristic Nectar Publications

Introduction

During the time of Emperor Nicholas I, there circulated a wide spread saying which stated that the Tsar attributed the stability of his Empire to three Philarets – 'Philaret of Moscow the wise, Philaret of Kiev the holy and Philaret of Chernigov the erudite.' Later all three hierarchs were canonized by the Russian Church.

It is meet and right that Saint Philaret of Moscow should be called the Chrysostom of the Church in the Russian land and it is a very desirable thing that his writings should become more familiar to Christians living in the West for the reviving of the gift of God in their life and for their edification into the mystery of Christ.

Saint Philaret writes that the word of God enlarges the heart, by igniting in it spiritual desire: 'Is your heart not pierced at Christ's teaching? Is not your heart enlarged to fit in all that is said?' The sermons of Saint Philaret, which are inspired by Holy Scripture and full of revelatory interpretations, must also be read in this same way, as his word is not the word of man but the word of God, which *effectively works in you who believe*. 1 Thessalonians 2:13

The word of God is born in the heart of those who have entered into His presence and spoken with Him, face to Face. When they return from this living presence of God, they find in their heart ready words, which they impart to their fellows. These words transmit grace, inform the hearts of them that hear them, and fashion their souls anew. These words are the language which God uses to speak to man and it is salutary for us to read them, because then we come to learn the language that we should use in order to speak to Him.

Saint Philaret of Moscow lived in the presence of God continually, and, coming out in order to speak with people, he would inform their hearts with grace. It is mentioned in his biography that he would always spend half the night in prayer. He was very devout in the serving of the Holy Liturgy and his blessed end occurred very soon after his last celebration. When we read his words, we learn how to present ourselves before God and our prayer gains wings.

However, if we do not uproot the law of sin from within us, and establish the law of the spirit as our foundation, accommodating in our heart the living sensation of the presence of God, then we shall never find any enduring source of inspiration. The words of Holy Scripture and the words of the Saints, inspired by the Holy Spirit, help us to continually rekindle the sensation of God within our heart. As these words come from a personal meeting with God, they contain the energy of His Person which is imparted to us.

Just as we must feed our body in order to survive, so also we need to be fed spiritually, with spiritual bread. This is the word of God, which is given to us in Holy Scripture, through the Holy Fathers and by the Holy Spirit directly into our heart. It is the bread of life, which will strengthen our heart to stand in the presence of God and to partake as well of the Bread of Life which descends from heaven, the Body and the Blood of the Lord Jesus. We continually need the spiritual bread of the word of God if we are to keep the covenant of love which we have concluded with Him in His Mysteries.

If we seek to apprehend the word of God directly, our heart must always be filled with the spirit of repentance. The gift of repentance is a preliminary gift, which leads us into the Church, but it is also the ultimate gift. In order for man to be able to apprehend the word of God, learn His language and speak to Him face to Face, he must have a heart burning with the spirit of repentance. Then, as Elder Sophrony says, all the being of man is contracted into one tight knot, so that he can turn himself entirely towards God and speak to Him with all his being. This is the state which meets with and fulfills the two great commandments, the basis of Christian life.

We cannot love God with all our heart and with all our being, if our heart is not ignited by the fire of repentance which Christ sent upon earth and longed to kindle in the hearts of all men. If man is not crushed and if his heart is not burning with the spirit of repentance, he cannot relate to God, the Father of mercies and the God of every comfort. The nature of the God of Christians is to be a Comforter, He never despises a broken and a contrite heart. He Himself says that He did not come to earth for those who are well, for those who have no need of healing. He came for those who are crushed and who seek the Face of God, as Elder Sophrony said, with deadly thirst. Such, he said, is the thirst of those who have perfected the spirit of repentance.

The word of God was given to us for consolation above all and it can only dwell in us when we are contrite. The word of Saint Philaret inspired and provoked contrition in the hearts of his listeners so they could be consoled and edified by the word of God.

We can neither understand the word of God when we read it, nor find contact with God in our prayer, nor feel the joy of prayer, unless we have a contrite spirit. As the word of God is light, and prayer with the Name of the Lord brings joy, both these prepare us to participate in the Mysteries wherein we find the power of God. We are enriched with light, joy and the power of God.

Saint Philaret was a sign of God for his generation, providing a word for his contemporaries and an answer to all their existential problems. We will only mention one concrete example, an exchange which began when Pushkin, the leading poet of his age, wrote some verses in deep despair, which, in a way, expressed that he was fighting with God:

> Vain gift, random gift
> Life, why have you been given to me?
> Or for what reason have you been
> Condemned to death by a secret fate?
>
> Who with inimical power
> Summoned me from nothingness
> Who filled my soul with passion
> Who disturbed my mind with doubt?
>
> No goal stands before me;
> My heart is empty,
> My mind idle,
> And the monotonous noise of life
> Wearies me with yearning.

Once published, these verses antagonized many within the Church, but then one Sunday the poet happened to go to a Liturgy served by Saint Philaret. When Philaret came out to preach, he saw Pushkin in the midst of his crowded congregation, and having read his verses, he started his sermon with a poem that he improvised at that moment:

> Not in vain and not by chance
> Has life been given to me by God,
> And it is not without God's mysterious will
> That I have been sentenced to punishment.
>
> It is I myself who, by my wayward use of power,
> Have brought forth evil from the dark depths,

> It is I myself who have filled my soul with suffering
> And my mind with anguishing doubt.
>
> Remember what you have forgotten!
> Let it shine through the twilight of thoughts –
> And through thee will be created
> a pure heart and a bright mind!

This poem of Saint Philaret had such a beneficial effect on Pushkin that he was inspired to write a further poem of gratitude and full of hope:

> In hours of amusement or idle boredom,
> Once upon a time, I used to confide
> To my lyre the cosseted sounds
> Of madness, indolence and passion.
>
> But even then I would arrest
> The vibration of the treacherous string
> When your majestic voice suddenly struck me.
>
> I poured forth streams of sudden tears,
> And to the wound of my conscience
> The balsam of your fragrant words
> Was a pure delight.
>
> And now from a spiritual height
> You extend a hand to me
> And with meek and loving strength
> Becalm restless dreams.
>
> Set afire by your flame my soul
> Has thrown off the darkness of earthly cares,
> And in a state of holy awe
> The poet listens to the harp of Philaret.

Reading the Holy Fathers anoints our mind with an anointing which removes the cursedness that we have gathered in this life and imparts to us the sense of the other world whence their words came to us.

The Russian earth gave birth to a cloud of holy Hierarchs, martyrs, great ascetics, righteous men and wonderworkers over many centuries – truly gifted and perfected spirits. However, it only gave birth to one Saint Philaret, of equal rank with the great hierarchs and ecumenical teachers, Saints Basil the Great, Gregory the Theologian and John Chrysostom. Saint Philaret alone had the outstanding charisma of the Holy Spirit for the building up of the Body of Christ, the holy and immaculate Church. He had a mind as deep as the Scriptures and possessed rare knowledge of the Mystery of Christ. He was the bearer of the spirit of Holy Scripture itself and of Orthodox Tradition. Above all, he was a biblical theologian, using Scripture to interpret Scripture. His word inspires and quickens the gift of every Christian, so that he can *hastening the coming of the day of God*. Then, finally, 'the day will dawn, and the day star arise' in the hearts of all those who loved 'the appearing' of our Lord Jesus Christ, to Whom belongs every glory and mighty love in the assembly of His Saints, among whom Saint Philaret shines as a bright star, the venerable enlightener of the faithful, our Father among the Saints, the Chrysostom of the Russian land.

2 Peter 3:12

Archimandrite Zacharias
Holy Stavropegic Monastery of St. John the Baptist
Essex, England
2019

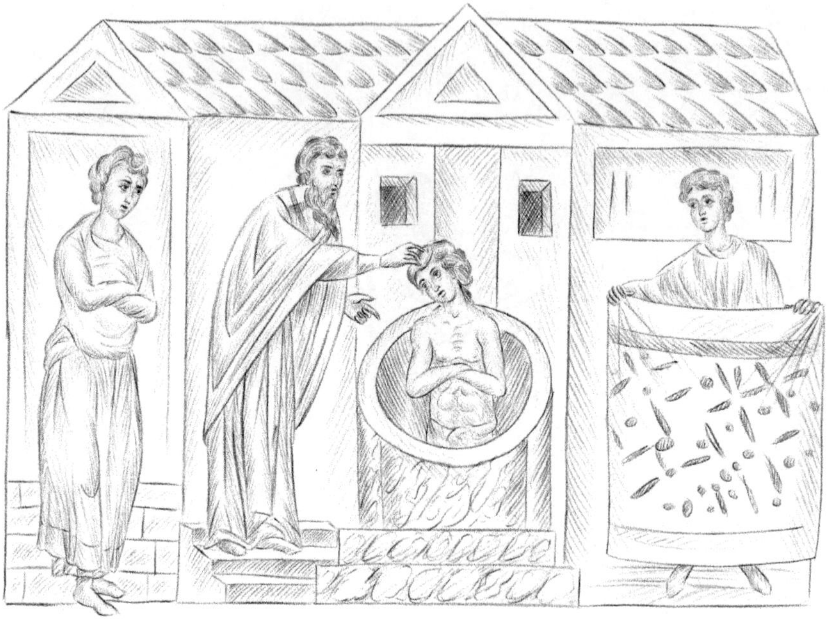

1

On Being Born Again (1844)

*"Do not marvel that I said to you,
'You must be born again.'" (John 3:7)*

It is not strange if the birth of some people, whose life will be especially pleasing to God and beneficial for other people, is both anticipated with an expectation of joy and is remembered with a feast. Thus, concerning the birth of the great Forerunner of the Lord, the angel prophesied: *Many will rejoice at his birth.* But when we see that the birthday of every person has become an occasion for a personal celebration, then thoughts of confusion and even astonishment arise.

Luke 1:14

Is a birthday a worthy subject for a celebration, considering that all of life is a rush toward death? As Job said, *Man who is born of woman is of few days and full of trouble.* Is that worth a celebration? David said, *Behold, I was brought forth in iniquity, and in sin my mother conceived me.* What is there to celebrate here? Blessed is he who is capable of celebrating the birth that erases our shortcomings, that corrects our imperfections, that ceases all the calamities of the first birth. This is the new birth, a birth in the Spirit, a birth from above.

Job 14:1

Psalm 50:5

You must be born again, said the Lord to Nicodemus during a solitary conversation at night. He did not use the singular when he told Nicodemus of the new birth, even though He spoke with only one man. He used the plural *you,* so that it would be obvious that the need to be born again is not a requirement for this or that person separately, but that this is a general rule for all who desire to be true disciples of the heavenly Teacher, Jesus Christ. *You* (plural) *must be born again.*

The Lord's teaching on man's rebirth seemed strange to Nicodemus, even though we cannot say that he was not well-intentioned, since he admitted that Jesus was sent by God. Neither can we say that he was ignorant, since he was a leader among the Pharisees. However, it was his carnal mindset that rose up at the beginning, considering subjects according to their worldly realities. And so, he asked, *How can a man be born when he is old?* *Can he enter a second time into his mother's womb and be born?* And when this crude, physical reasoning was rejected by the exalted understanding of the higher birth through water and the Spirit, then he graduated from a carnal to a philosophical mindset, requiring explanation and proof: *How can these things be?*

John 3:4

John 3:9

Is it not similar in our time? What is rebirth? What a strange thought—how can man, during the course of his existence, be produced anew, when he, without a doubt, must remain one and the same person? What is the point of this esoteric reasoning, this opaque mysteriousness? Isn't it enough just to be a good Christian? Do not such words against the profound teaching of Christianity sometimes burst forth from the mouths of some, like stones that are thrown thoughtlessly, without realizing they might hurt someone?

Know this: here we speak not about some private, self-aggrandizing opinion, for I desire, together with the apostle, for *Everyone who is among you, not to think of himself more highly than he ought to think, but to think soberly, as God has dealt to each one a measure of faith*. I do not speak of a passion for esoteric, dark mysteries (in any case, I do not understand why anyone would prefer mystery to clarity), nor do I speak of any kind of departure from simplicity, for I care for simplicity, as did the apostle: *I fear, lest somehow...your minds may be corrupted from the simplicity that is in Christ*. On the contrary, I speak of a most important reality—to find or to lose the kingdom of God. Rebirth is not required to make a person a wise man or an initiate into esoteric mysteries, but to acquire the kingdom of God. If you refuse to accept the thought of rebirth, then you distance yourself from the chance to see the kingdom of God: *Most assuredly, I say to you, unless one is born again, he cannot see the kingdom of God*. And so, I repeat: blessed is he who is able to celebrate his second birth from above.

Romans 12:3

2 Corinthians 11:3

John 3:3

Perhaps you will answer thus: "Why do we not congratulate each other with the blessedness of being born anew when we are born with the water and Spirit in holy baptism?" This is a thought worthy of attentive contemplation and investigation into the teaching concerning rebirth.

Let us differentiate baptism by water and baptism by the Spirit, as Jesus Christ Himself differentiated them in His words to the Apostles: *For John truly baptized with water, but you shall be baptized with the Holy Spirit not many days from now*. And so let us ask, "Have we only been baptized with water, not the Spirit?" No, without a doubt! If it were only a baptism by water, then it would be no different from any physical ablutions required during the times of the Old Testament. It would be a rite, and would not deserve the name "sacrament" — a name which it is, in fact, given by the Church. In that case, the lordly name of the Father and the Son and the Holy Spirit would be strangely ineffectual in baptism. To insist that we were baptized in the name of the Holy Spirit, but did not receive the baptism of the Spirit, would be an unresolvable contradiction.

Acts 1:5

For as many of you as were baptized into Christ have put on Christ. [Galatians 3:27] Without a doubt, water cannot do this, only the Spirit. However, if our baptism is more than just a washing with water, then we cannot fail to admit that it is the baptism of both water and Spirit, or, as the Lord said, a birth by water and Spirit. Or, in the words of the Apostle, *the washing of regeneration.* [Titus 3:5] In short, it is a new birth. Thus, truly have we received new life through baptism, *having been born again, not of corruptible seed but incorruptible, through the word of God which lives and abides forever* [1 Peter 1:23] by the power of the name of the Father and the Son and the Holy Spirit.

So? Is the kingdom of God, then, truly within us? It must be so. So, are we blessed? Let anyone who can say that about himself. However, I do not dare to say this, for I see too much in myself that contradicts this statement. I see more deeds and phenomena of the unborn man within me, the old man, not the reborn, new man. I see more of the poverty of Adam than the blessedness of Christ.

Let us see how the Holy Scriptures describe the qualities of the truly reborn man.

Whoever has been born of God does not sin, for His seed remains in him; and he cannot sin, because he has been born of God. [1 John 3:9] In other words, the grace of God, like a seed, like the principle of a new life in man, gives him inspiration of hope and love for God, which constantly produces good thoughts, intentions, and deeds in him. Therefore, it is unnatural for him to commit sin and to find pleasure in it. Can any of us baptized Christians say this about ourselves?

For whatever is born of God overcomes the world. [1 John 5:4] Do any of us feel ourselves to be triumphant over the world? Are not many of us defeated by avarice, glory, by the vanity of the world? Are not many of us slaves of sin's pleasure?

The Apostle John wrote, *But you have an anointing from the Holy One, and you know all things. And you do not need that anyone teach* [1 John 2:20] *you; but as the same anointing teaches you concerning all things, and is true, and is not a lie, and just as it has taught you, you will abide in Him.* Show me here at least one man who knows everything, so that I can learn from him how to resolve the difficulty of this teaching of the Apostle.

1 John 2:27

We now stand between two extremes. On the one hand, there are reasons to believe that we are communicants of spiritual regeneration through holy baptism. On the other hand, there are clear indications that force us to admit that we simply lack the majority of the qualities and actions of a born-again person. How can we explain or resolve this contradiction?

Here the words of the parable are fitting: *The kingdom of heaven is like treasure hidden in a field.* The field is a symbol of man. The depths in which the treasure symbolizes the heart or the inner part of man, which is more or less opened up by faith. It is here that the Spirit of God, who *blows where [He] wishes,* has breathed invisibly. Through this breath, He has brought into our depths a treasure, an incorruptible seed of rebirth, a new life from God. And so, the treasure has been buried, and truly is in our field. But has every one of us done everything required by the parable? Have we found the treasure through profound self-examination and by entering deep within ourselves? Have we hidden that treasure from the invisible robbers by humility? Have we sold all that we have, have we rejected the world and the flesh, and have we abandoned every vestige of passion and desire to become able to take the inner treasure and use it for our personal blessedness? If we have done none of this, if we have not taken any pains to go deep within to find the hidden treasure of our heart; if we have remained only on the surface of the field, taking pleasure in physical things as a beast that feeds on plants; if we have buried our hidden treasure deeper and deeper by heaping the garbage and refuse of our vain, impure, lawless thoughts and deeds—then the treasure remains buried, but we do not use

Matthew 13:44

John 3:8

it. The incorruptible seed within us does not sprout or flower or bear fruit. Our spiritual life is either in fetal stage or in a comatose state.

We have to want someone to care for our rebirth, as St. Paul worried for the rebirth of the Galatians whom he had baptized: *My little children, for whom I labor in birth again until Christ is formed in you...* Paul's labor pains are not for the first time. At first, he labored to place a seed of the Spirit into their hearts by faith and baptism (*Having begun in the Spirit, are you now being made perfect in the flesh?*). Then, he labored in pain to reveal the spiritual treasure, buried under the predominating flesh, to help the stunted shoot of the Spirit blossom until it was able to bear spiritual fruits so that the image of Christ impressed on the spirit by baptism would be revealed in all its capabilities, powers, disposition, and Christ-like and God-pleasing deeds. *I labor in birth again [for you] until Christ is formed in you...*

Galatians 4:19

Galatians 3:3

Galatians 4:19

Whoever agrees with these thoughts concerning the importance and necessity of every Christian's being born again, but at the same time does not obtain a comforting witness of his deeds and conscience concerning the fruits of rebirth—such a person must consider, not without care, the state that he is in, and where this state will lead. The judgment of Christ has been uttered and, truly, it will not change. As He judged during a silent night in the presence of Nicodemus alone, so also will He judge in the glorious final day, in the presence of all the angels and all men. He who is not born again cannot see the kingdom of God!

Others may think, "Can we decisively determine all the ways to the kingdom of heaven? Perhaps, somehow, we will be saved as well?" This is similar to a person who, seeing the difficulties and vagaries of agriculture, said, "Maybe wheat will grow without my working the land or sowing it." As the Apostle said, *He who sows to the Spirit will of the Spirit reap everlasting life.* If we do not sow, truly, we will reap nothing.

Galatians 6:8

Or perhaps yet another person may say, "Very well. I will definitely sow in the Spirit, and I will immediately be reborn." No, beloved! This is not a trustworthy path. Neither a careless "maybe" nor a self-assured "definitely" is worth anything in the work of the Spirit. Whoever thinks his rebirth can be made on command will become only a useless dreamer. A child cannot be born whenever and however he wishes. His mother must give birth to him, as is the way of nature. In the same way, no person can be reborn whenever and however he wishes. The Spirit of God must give him new birth, as is the way of grace.

Between the extremes of careless inactivity and self-assured brazenness lies the humble but active way of the Spirit, which the Apostle describes in the following words: *Work out your own salvation with fear and trembling.* Work out your salvation, but do not think that it will be worked out by itself. Instead, do it with fear and trembling, never trusting in anything that you yourself are able to do, and constantly being careful lest you hinder God's own activity within you, *for it is God who works in you both to will and to do for His good pleasure.*

Philippians 2:12

Philippians 2:13

Would you like to know what most depends on us in the work of rebirth, what is most necessary from us? Look at the Apostle's image of physical birth, symbolizing birth by the Spirit. It is not only the mother who suffers during labor, but the baby being born also suffers and cries. This is a living parable for the teaching concerning the second birth. You must labor in pain through your old, physical life, which you have not yet abandoned. Cry for your sins, not only because hell awaits you because of them, but even more so because you were not faithful to God who created you and who loves you. Cry that you have been found ungrateful before Christ who suffered for you. Cry because you have sorrowed the Holy Spirit. Cry with heartfelt tears, tears of sorrowful love. Find nourishment in your tears, as it is written, *My tears have been my bread day and night. For godly sorrow produces repentance leading to salvation, not to be regretted.* This repentance must

Psalm 41:4

2 Corinthians 7:10

not be only verbal, but active; not short-lived, but constant and resolute. This repentance must be the kind that in the baptized is significantly called "a second baptism," and, therefore, an essential part of the new birth that will bring joy in heaven.

Come to know the spiritual taste of pure, divine sorrow, all you who seek to be children of God. And then, you will come to know rebirth, and you will taste new life, for your own joy and for the joy of those in heaven – complete joy that will never be taken away from you. Amen.

2

On Gratitude to God (1842)

*We...plead with you not to receive
the grace of God in vain. (2 Corinthians 6:1)*

The Apostle Paul explained to his Corinthian disciples the greatest of God's gifts to mankind—the redemption from the domain of sin by the Only-begotten Son of God's descent into that domain. By this descent, He destroyed the evil and death-bearing power of sin by the all-encompassing and all-powerful, life-giving, and beneficent power of God. *For He made Him who knew no sin to be sin for us, that we might become the righteousness of God in Him.* Having explained this greatest of God's gifts, the holy Apostle immediately added an exhortation, which, due to his love for these disciples and the strength of his desire that they heed his words, he gave in the form of a request: *We...plead with you not to receive the grace of God in vain.*

2 Corinthians 5:21

2 Corinthians 6:1

Are we not also all the recipients of this grace of God indicated by the Apostle, O brother Christians? Therefore, I have the same responsibility to repeat to you these words of the Apostle:

"We plead with you not to receive the grace of God in vain." I beg you that the gifts that you have received, and continue to receive from God, will not be received in vain. Show yourselves to be faithful to His grace, worthy of His gifts. Let us explain this in more detail.

Man lives by the unending gifts of God. He is comprised completely of the gifts and benevolence of God. He is submerged in the gifts of God as in an abyss.

The existence and life of a person, in its beginning, is the free gift of the Creator. It is a gift that no one could have forced Him to give, that no one had the right to demand of Him. Consequently, the continuation of that existence and life is also a constant continuation of that same gift of God. Every minute of this temporary life is a gift from God. And man's immortality is the immortal, eternal gift of God.

Let us consider what we are made of. The soul, the foundation of our life, is the breath of God the Creator. The body, the house and instrument of the soul, is the work of God's hands. The mind, without which you would have no truth, no wisdom; and the heart, without which you would have no good, no blessedness, no emotion, without which the cosmos that surrounds you would be closed and inaccessible to you—is not all of this also God's word, God's gift to you who are a worthless bit of nothing? Truly, you are made completely from the gifts and benevolence of God.

Let us look around at the world. Who laid the ground under our feet, which holds us above the abyss, which gives us a home, clothing, and food? Who poured water on this earth, which nourishes us and washes us? Who lit the luminaries in the heavens, which give us the possibility to see the world with its miracles, which draws forth life for us from the dead earth, beauty, sweet smells and tastes, food, medicines, and which feeds our own lives with subtle, but no less earthly, nourishment? Whose air do we breathe? Who instituted the day, which inspires us to activity, and the night, which gives us needed rest? Who gave to the wheat its natural law, whereby from only a few seeds, necessary for the continuation of the species, it brings forth great multitudes of fruit for our bread? Who commanded the tree to bring forth far more seeds for us than it needs for itself? Who commanded the proud horse to humble itself under our heaviness, or the humble sheep, or even the smallest worm to weave from its own silk clothing for our use? Who prepared fire for us, for times when the sun hides itself, to come sparking out of the flint and steel or the wood and oil? Is not all this, and so many other uncountable things, all God's dispensation, God's property, and when it is given for our benefit, God's beneficence? Truly, we are submerged in the benevolence of God as in an abyss.

Perhaps one who is inattentive to the benevolence of God will say, "I use that which I find in my nature and in the surrounding nature, thanks to my own exertions or with the help of others. I have worked, sought, produced, and invented." To such a person we answer together with the Apostle, *Neither he who plants is anything, nor he who waters, but God who gives the increase.* Paul's rebuke of the uselessness of human works compared to the beneficent cooperation of God with respect to the cultivation of visible nature is a fair metaphor for God's cultivation of the spiritual nature in man. You dug a trench or a hole, you threw some seed there or planted a root, and maybe even sprinkled the ground with water (if in a small garden). What limited, dead, worthless actions! But what, at the same time, is the work of the heavenly Husbandman? He invisibly (and amazingly) prepared the future plant in the seed or in the root. The ground, into which you threw the seed as into a tomb, He also prepared as a mother's womb. Later, it is He who commands the sun to break through the dark and cold clods of earth with light and warmth and to pull out a shoot from the buried seed, and from the shoot a stem, and from the stem a flower and a fruit. To aid this process, it is He who once again sends alternately cold then heat, and humidity then dryness, and rain and dew, and winds and calm.

1 Corinthians 3:7

Naturally, it is not man who plants and nourishes, but God. He uses earth, water, air, and light to produce the potential of bread within the stalk of wheat and the potential of wine in the grape. And yet, see how strange we are! We bring much attention to our own work, but precisely because it is so limited! We say that we begin our work and finish it, that we labor at it and are tired from it. But, on the contrary, we never bring attention to the blessings of God, precisely because they are so great! Because they are ready without labor, because they are ubiquitous, even quotidian. Sometimes, a temporary and local loss of the benevolent hand of God is necessary for people to correctly value the gifts of God that they had used for so long without any attentiveness. Thus, for example, famine is excellent at explaining God's blessing of bread; a plague reminds us of the blessing of good air; droughts remind us of the blessing of rain; inclement weather reminds us of the gift of the sun, which is only not valued by us because the all-good God shines His sun every day both on the evil and the good.

When we look at human society, the thought of the beneficent hand of God is often hindered by the thought of the free will of man. However, can God, the benevolent Creator of the world and man, not also be the benevolent Creator of human society? For a society of men that was independent of Him and not directed by Him would prevent Him from fulfilling His benevolent intentions concerning the world and mankind. Such a situation would limit God, which contradicts the very nature of divinity.

No one who admits God to be Creator and Provider will even begin to argue that the societies of bees or ants are not directed by the hand of God in nature, because no individual member of a beehive ever came up with a theory for bee societies. No ant philosopher ever invented fables concerning social contracts. Well? Is human society less worthy to be structured by the all-wise God and be a constant subject of His beneficent direction? Yes, human beings rule over other human beings. However, that in no

SERMON 2: ON GRATITUDE TO GOD

way contradicts that each of them has, by nature, a free will. In the same way, the existence of this free will in no way contradicts the existence of the overarching rule of God over the human race, over every individual family, and over every government.

This rule of God is not inactive merely because it is invisible; and God, without a doubt, has the means to achieve His ends more effectively than any human government. As soon as we come to believe that our natural state, as well as the state of our society, is under the all-good and all-wise direction of God, then everything good and benevolent in our life—good parents, wise teachers, illumined mentors, just judges, solicitous superiors, and all the more so our wise and benevolent Tsar, and his successes, and good intentions for his government, victory over enemies, destruction of revolt, the acquisition, preservation, and confirmation of peace, the improvement of public services—all this only increases the never-ending list of the gifts and blessings of the King of kings, the Lord of lords, the Father *from whom the whole family in heaven and earth is named*. *Ephesians 3:15*

I shall sing of Thy mercy, O Lord, for ever, exclaimed the Psalmist, *Psalm 88:2* proclaiming his praise of the covenant of God to David as King and Patriarch, a promise that brings good things for the kingdom and the people. He also prays for a renewal of these ancient mercies of the Lord. If anyone here thinks that this is how it was, but only for the Hebrews, then I say to you together with the Apostle: *Or is He the God of the Jews only? Is He not also the God of the Gentiles? Yes, of the Gentiles also*. Is our God the God who blesses the *Romans 3:29* kingly rule only of the Jews? No, but of all Christians as well. Yes, even Russians!

However, no matter how many or how great the gifts of God to man in his natural and social life, far greater, more important, more countless, and more indescribable are His blessings that refer to the spiritual and eternal life of man. The former two (natural and societal) kinds of blessings can only be counted as preparatory and as aiding the latter. The former creates existence out of nothingness and gives order to existence. The latter gives a sinner blamelessness, a condemned man his release, a spiritually dead person new life, and salvation and blessedness to the lost. In the former, created matter is prepared and used for the benefit of created beings. But in the latter, the Creator Himself comes to help His creation. He comes to serve creation. He gives it Himself. The Son of God is not spared, but is betrayed for the sake of all. The flesh and blood of the God-Man is offered as food and drink, as medicine, as the source of life. God's heart opens up; the love of God pours forth into our hearts. The Holy Spirit is given. Many mansions in heaven open their doors for those born on earth, and the very heart of man is made into a dwelling place of God. Whoever understands that the soul of man can only truly live in God, as the body lives only while the soul is in it, but also that God cannot live in an impure soul; whoever has enough self-knowledge to see how miserably and how almost inevitably the delusion of the Serpent and the enticement of Eve repeat in us through pride of mind and lust of flesh; how every unrighteous deed, even every impure desire or evil thought, cast the soul out of the paradise of a peaceful conscience; how, finally, our own efforts are insufficient to rise out of the hell of a wounded conscience—such a person understands at least somewhat how great is the gift of the grace of redemption, purification, and forgiveness. He understands how wondrous is the gift of even remaining in a state of grace.

As for the higher gifts of grace—illumination, sanctification, union with God—concerning these things, even he who has come to know the other gifts of God can say so little, since he has only seen a small gift of alms, as a coin given to a poor man in the street. He can say nothing concerning the generous, precious, sweet gifts that the King gives in the inner sanctum of His court to His intimates, that the Master of the house gives to His friends, that the love-filled Father gives His eternal children.

I now stop this summary of God's gifts not because I have said enough, but because one can never say enough. I now stop and I listen. What will your consciences say to me in answer? How do your hearts respond?

Is there truly a special way that man must relate to God, his Benefactor? Is there some kind of reciprocation required of us? Or perhaps nothing is required of us? I don't think anyone would ever say that. If there is someone who would, then I doubt that he even has a heart in his chest, but rather a cold and hard stone, or a sponge that hungrily drinks someone else's water without actually thirsting or tasting or being satisfied. Does he even have a mind in his head? Or perhaps it's something worse than bestial instinct, since at least "the ox knows its owner and the donkey its master's crib." (Isaiah 1:3) Even the irrational beasts know man by his benevolence, and act toward him accordingly.

But if we must act in a way that relates to God's blessings, then what does it consist of? Paying back a service, further requests, or gratitude—here are three possible responses to benevolence. Paying back a service is only possible between people who each need the other's services. In such a situation, one may pay back the other's good deed with his own. But the perfect God has need of nothing, and man has nothing to offer God in return. Consequently, paying back a service has no place in the relationship between man and God.

As for further requests, yes, it is possible and even good to ask God for further blessings, but only if man does it with trust and with humility. But the greater part of God's blessings are given to us before we even ask for them, or in a better way than we imagined to ask, or even surpassing our understanding. We cannot ask for something that is already given. Nor can we ask for something that is not in our thoughts. Therefore, the best way to relate to God's gifts is gratitude, as true as God's gifts are true; as active as God's benevolence to us is active.

Therefore, *we plead with you not to receive the grace of God in vain.* Show yourselves faithful to the grace of God in your heart. Show yourselves to be worthy of His grace in actual fact. Did the Lord perform a sign in your life by delivering you from harm or danger? Remembering what happened, put your trust only in the Lord in the future, and use this grace for your benefit in the present moment. Has God extended His hand in generosity by giving you earthly riches? Extend your own grateful hand to help your destitute neighbor. Has the benevolent providence of God revealed itself in a good Tsar, in a rule of law that preserves peace in our life? Let us raise our gratitude to the King of kings through our joyful doxologies and in sincere prayer for His anointed one. Let us reveal fruits of gratitude in our zealous fulfillment of any duties we are given in this life.

Have you found in your heart the gift of the grace of God—the forgiveness of your sins, the peace of your conscience, and the joy of your salvation? Then thank God with firm and constantly renewed determination to flee from sin, with a profound attention to your inner world to preserve the peace of your conscience, with a meek but unflagging energy to aid the salvation of your neighbors.

Has the heavenly Founder of labors found anyone worthy of the honor of a cross, the labor of temptations, sorrows, or sufferings? Let such a man understand that even a punishment from the all-good Father is a gift, and that this particular gift is *for our profit, that we may be partakers of His holiness.* Therefore, let us learn not to complain or lose faith, but to praise the name of the Lord together with Job or the Psalmist: *It is good for me that Thou didst humble me, that I may learn Thy statutes.*

Give thanks for everything, *for this is the will of God in Christ Jesus for you.* Amen.

3

On the Fear of God (1844)

"Therefore, since we are receiving a kingdom which cannot be shaken, let us have grace, by which we may serve God acceptably with reverence and godly fear." (Hebrews 12:28)

The Apostle Paul wrote this exhortation to Christian converts from Judaism, but the Holy Spirit who spoke through Paul passed on these words as an instruction to Christians of all peoples and times, and consequently, to us as well.

Since the Apostle applies his words not merely to authorities but to all Christians in general, then we can conclude that "receiving a kingdom which cannot be shaken" means taking part not in kingly authority but in the advantages and goods of a higher kingdom.

The *grace* of which the Apostle here speaks, which is not given by God to man but by man to God, evidently here means "gratitude."

Due to these observations, the reasoning behind the apostolic exhortation is as follows: if the goodness of God gives us participation in the advantages and benefits of an unconquerable kingdom, then we must have gratitude to God in our hearts, and, due to this feeling of gratitude, we must serve Him in a way that pleases Him, with reverence and fear.

Hearkening to this apostolic encouragement to be grateful before God, which must become a proper service to God, let us not fail to bring attention to the quality of grateful service to God that the apostolic word demands of us. "We may serve God acceptably with reverence and godly fear."

Here, we must explore in more detail the foundation of the apostolic commandments. First, he said, *But you have come to Mount Zion and to the city of the living God, the heavenly Jerusalem, to an innumerable company of angels, to the general assembly and church of the firstborn who are registered in heaven.* Then, based on that thought, he offers the following conclusion: *Therefore, since we are receiving a kingdom which cannot be shaken, let us have grace, by which we may serve God.* From this, it is clear that the kingdom we speak of here is the eternal blessedness of the kingdom of heaven. And if this is the kingdom we have in mind, and if we even accept it, and by this acceptance are inspired to be grateful and to serve gratefully before God, then, it seems to me, it would be most logical to demand that we serve God with hope, with joy, and with gladness. But this is not how the Apostle reasons. He says, *that we may serve God acceptably with reverence and godly fear.*

Hebrews 12:22

Hebrews 12:28

Hebrews 12:28

These words of the Apostle can seem even more wondrous to us if we remember that in other circumstances, fear is a state proper to a slave who lives under the law of the Old Testament, a state that one might think is foreign to a Christian who lives under the grace of the New Testament: *For you did not receive the spirit of bondage again to fear, but you received the Spirit of adoption by whom we cry out, 'Abba, Father.'* And also: *For God has not given us a spirit of fear, but of power and of love and of a sound mind.* Similarly, another of the Apostles speaks of fear as something inferior, something of which we will be eventually freed: *Perfect love casts*

Romans 8:15

2 Timothy 1:7

out fear, because fear involves torment. But he who fears has not been made perfect in love.   *1 John 4:18*

How can we reconcile such different opinions on the same subject? And should we not be afraid as we strive toward perfect love to leave fear behind, and consequently to break the commandment concerning service to God with fear? Or, on the contrary, perhaps we should fear that if we hold on to fear, we will hold ourselves back in our ascent toward the perfection of love?

These questions show that this invitation of the triumphant Leader does not only refer to small children: *Come, ye children, and hearken unto me; I will teach you the fear of the Lord.* I don't think that *Psalm 33:12* it's necessary to teach, in general terms, what is the fear of God. It is evident enough from simple experience. If you can understand the fear of a slave before a king, the fear of a justly condemned man before his judge, then you merely have to increase the comparison until it can no longer be measured, and then you can understand what man's fear of God should be.

But in order to avoid confusion, we must distinguish the forms of this fear and the different degrees to which it rises or falls in different people or in different inner states of a single person. Lest these distinctions seem arbitrary, we will cite the words of the Apostles. *For you did not receive the spirit of bondage again to fear.*   *Romans 8:15* Thus, there is a kind of fear that we can safely call "slavish," and to this we can contrast the "filial" kind of fear. Slavish fear in the service of God is an inner state that fears a God who punishes sins, and therefore turns away and flees from sin and everything else that is abhorrent to God. A filial fear is an internal disposition of the soul that loves God with reverence, as an all-good Father, and fears to offend Him because it loves Him. The highest degree of filial fear is a "pure fear," completely imbued with love, and freed totally from slavish fear. On the contrary, the lowest form of slavish fear is the fear of a *wicked and lazy servant*. This   *Matthew 25:26* is an inner state in which a person is not so much afraid of God as he is afraid of the pain of the punishment for sin, and so although he serves God externally, he does not hate sin, nor does he labor to extirpate it for the sake of virtue. He is always ready to abandon himself to sin again, as soon as he imagines it to be not so dangerous that it will result in eternal punishment.

After making these distinctions, it is not hard to determine and reconcile the meanings of the various cases of the "fear of God" that we find in the Scriptures. If the Apostle tells us Christians that "God has not given us a spirit of fear," then, without a doubt, he means here the fear of a slave, not the fear of a son, a fear that is appropriate for a "Spirit of adoption" because it is also one of the movements of the same Spirit. In a similar way, if a different Apostle said that "perfect love casts out fear," then here he clearly speaks of slavish fear. Love has no need to cast out filial, pure fear, for it is animated by love. Anything that is pure is not subject to rejection, which is why the Scriptures speak of a pure fear of the Lord, and say that it abides forever.

Psalm 18:10

To remain at the level of fear of punishment would, without a doubt, be demeaning for a Christian. He must labor to purify his fear, to ascend from slavish to filial fear. However, the opposite is also true. If someone says that he wants to be led by the Spirit of filial fear, but does not work on removing his slavish fear, or if he pretends to only be subject to perfected love, without first working through slavish fear—such a person is brazen in his thoughts, and he is not far from perdition. God gave you a spirit of sonship, but He did not say to you, "Fear no more." Even the beloved Disciple of the Lord, the herald of perfected love, does not mention casting out all fear from your heart. He only reveals the mystery of perfection, and that perfected love, when it comes, casts out fear without your exertion, without even your participation, and, perhaps, without you even realizing it. He also does not say that the fear will never return; after all, while love casts out fear so that man can taste the sweetness of the triumph of grace, humility calls fear back, lest the grace-filled man forget his unworthiness. And if you yourself cast out fear, then who will lead you to love? Because, as the Wise One said, "The fear of the Lord places one on the path to love."[1]

Who brought divine sonship to earth and gifted it to mankind? Was it not the Only-begotten Son of God, who was incarnate for this reason, and who freed us by His blood from the slavery to sin? Did He not grant the freedom of being sons of God to those who were burdened down with the fear of death? Well? Did He free us from the necessity of having fear of God? On the contrary! He Himself preached it more powerfully and more insistently than any of His disciples: *My friends, do not be afraid of those who kill the body, and after that have no more that they can do. But I will show you whom you should fear. Fear Him who, after He has killed, has power to cast into hell; yes, I say to you, fear Him!*   *Luke 12:4-5*

Therefore, let us not be astonished when St. Paul, who himself knew perfected love and professed sonship to God, commanded us to serve God with fear. Let us take more care to fulfill this commandment than to examine it. Active fulfillment, much more than examination, will prove the commandment's worth, power, and effectiveness.

If the fear of God leads you to come to church to serve God, then it will not fail to bring you here as on wings. It will place you here, truly before the face of God. It will open your mind to be profoundly attentive to the word of God, and your heart to accept the grace of the Mysteries. It will not allow your thoughts or your gaze to wander all over the earth when they should instead be directed toward heaven, from where we expect help, and from where help comes. Fear of God will not allow us to waste this blessed conversation with God for the sake of idle talk with other people. It will make our participation in the service both God-pleasing and sweet and nourishing for our souls.

---

1   In the Russian original, this is quoted as Sirach 1:13 (Masoretic). However, the LXX has a different reading.

If the fear of God accompanies you out of the church into your daily and social life, then it will be a trustworthy guard against dangerous meetings, a firm wall against the enemy's arrows, and a humble advocate for exalted good things.

Do you fear the enticement of sin? *The beginning of wisdom is the fear of the Lord.* And not only the beginning, but *the fear of the Lord is the crown of wisdom.*

<small>Proverbs 1:7</small>
<small>Sirach 1:16</small>

Are you in danger of calamity or death? *He who fears the Lord will fear nothing, and he will not be cowardly, for the Lord is his hope. The command of the Lord is a fountain of life, for it causes one to turn from the snare of death.*

<small>Sirach 34:14</small>
<small>Proverbs 14:28</small>

What man is he, that feareth the Lord? To him shall He give a Law in the way which He hath chosen. His souls shall dwell at ease, and his seed shall inherit the land. The Lord is the strength of them that fear Him, and He will show them His covenant.

<small>Psalm 24:12-14</small>

Only with the fear of God can your labor be lawful, your hope be sure, and your joy be without danger. Therefore, it is said, *Serve the Lord in fear, and rejoice unto Him with trembling.*

<small>Psalm 2:11</small>

Even if you are saints, it is still said of the saints, *O fear the Lord, all ye that are His saints.* If you do not dare to ascribe this dignity to yourselves, then all the more you must *work out your own salvation with fear and trembling, perfecting holiness in the fear of God.* Amen.

<small>Psalm 33:10</small>
<small>Philippians 2:12</small>
<small>2 Corinthians 7:1</small>

4

On Pious Zeal (1832)

*"Not lagging in diligence, fervent in spirit,
serving the Lord." (Romans 12:11)*

It is not merely St. Paul who inspires me to speak about pious zeal with his God-inspired teaching. It is also the example of the great hosts of saints.

Those who have gathered here, perhaps inspired by pious zeal, will be encouraged to hear something that so agrees with the witness of their own conscience. In general, no one should consider anything that the Apostle of Christ teaches to be of little importance or merely tangential for one's own salvation.

Not lagging in diligence, fervent in spirit, serving the Lord. By the last of these three, the Apostle exhorts us to actively fulfill our responsibilities to God. By the first two, he determines with what spiritual disposition we must fulfill those duties. *Romans 12:11*

The work of a slave is to labor for his master. It is the same for a Christian—he must labor for the Lord. In what way? He must labor over his mind, to illumine it by the knowledge of the truth of God and His holy will. He must labor over his heart to purify it of passions and impure desires, that it may become a worthy sacrifice to God and a receptacle of His grace. He must labor with all his strength and abilities to do everything for God in a manner pleasing to God. In other words, he must honorably discharge the duties of his calling for God; he must give alms to the poor for His sake; he must patiently endure sorrows for His glory. Earthly masters are content only with the kind of work that brings gain, and naturally they don't consider the requests or kind words of their slaves and hirelings to be of equal value with work that brings profit. But the heavenly Master does not seek from us any sort of personal gain, for He has no need of it. He accepts our work only to provide us with good things. He accepts our prayers and doxologies to Him as a service and labor that pleases Him.

From this, it is not difficult to see how multifaceted is labor for the Lord, and how it extends throughout the entire life of both the inner and outer man, until the Great Sabbath—the final rest in God Himself. It would be very bad if such labor were accomplished without effort or with laziness. The lazy one does not do what he must; the indolent does everything so-so, not worrying about success or doing his work well. Such laborers are considered worthless by earthly masters. How much more worthless are they before the eyes of the heavenly Master. Therefore, the loyal Watchman of the Lord's works calls to all who labor for Him, "Do not lag in diligence!" Do not be lazy or lacking in effort! But, not content with this, he adds the following: "Be ardent in spirit!" Have a spirit on fire, a fiery zeal, a boiling eagerness to serve God and to do His will.

An ardent zeal toward God is a quality that means much in a Christian's character, both in determining what he will be and how much he can accomplish.

First of all, zeal is that which makes any labor for the Lord's sake pleasing to God. This can be explained simply and proved by your own experience. You light a candle before the holy icon, and by this you intend a kind of service before God. But you know that neither God nor His Saints, who abide in the heavenly mansions of the Holy of Holies, have any need of an earthly, physical candle. You see that you could probably do without these candles sometimes in church, illumined as it is by God's great light in the sky. So what does the lighting of a candle mean, and how can it be pleasing to God and His Saints? It only pleases God when it is a visible symbol of your own ardent spirit, your own pious zeal. The Spirit of God determined the various forms of service in the Church according to rank and ability. The priest prays, glorifies, performs the mysteries, and teaches. The lesser clergy inspire others to prayer and spiritual knowledge by their sacred reading or singing, by describing the rite or explaining the reason for our prayers. You, who stand in silence and listen must become inspired, lest you seem to be separated from active participation in the service, a worthless member of the Church; to *you* is given the symbolic action of lighting a candle before the holy icon. When you do this, your conscience is convinced that you are participating in service to God, and the Church is comforted, seeing by this sign that you are ardent in spirit and that God is pleased by the sacrifice of your heart.

This example should also help illumine other pious actions. Man does not see the heart of his neighbor. However, he is not content with appearances and the superficial alone. He tries by signs to guess whether or not an action is performed with eagerness. And when he finds such zeal, he highly prizes the action and is much consoled. Therefore, can God, the Knower of hearts, ever be content with only the visible and superficial manifestation of piety and virtue when he does not see in a man's heart the corresponding pious zeal? "Give me your heart," says His Wisdom to man. And correspondingly, *The Lord grant thee according to thy heart.* Christ judged the heart of the widow of Jerusalem when she put two coppers into the Temple's treasury, and His

Psalm 19:50

judgment was that her gift was greater than all the others. Pious zeal makes a small, worthless coin priceless to God.

Secondly, pious zeal helps a man do the work of the Lord. It lessens the burden of service to God. It speeds up his steps along the road to spiritual perfection. When a man of the world and the flesh hears the commandments that must govern a godly man's life—do not love the world or what is of the world, reject your riches, that is, give them away to the poor, or use them with the same indifference as though you did not have them, and moderate your love for your father, mother, wife, and children, lest you love them more than you love God, and take up your cross—he is horrified by the heaviness of the Lord's work. He cannot understand how anyone can bear such a burden.

Against this, the all-powerful Establisher of labors said, *For My yoke is easy, and My burden is light.* But not only God, but His servant, equally sinful to us, also said, *His commandments are not burdensome.* How are we to resolve the seeming discrepancy with the apparent difficulty and the actual ease? The resolution is found in a proper understanding of pious zeal. *I ran the way of thy commandments, when Thou didst enlarge my heart.* Through this, the Psalmist lets us know that the way of God's commandments, the way of a pious and spiritual life, only seems difficult, and a person only deviates from it, vacillates, stumbles, and is unable to lift his feet as long as his heart is constricted, cold, and uninspired to do good. But when his heart expands with spiritual ardor, and when it becomes aroused with divine desire, then man runs along God's path easily and quickly.

The experienced ascetic knows this, and if you want to understand, pay attention to how important an ardent spirit is in everyday life. I will give you an example. Jacob gave himself to Laban as a laborer for seven years. Instead of payment, he asked for Rachel in marriage: *So Jacob served seven years for Rachel, and they seemed only a few days to him because of the love he had for her.* Rachel, who was beautiful to look at, is also a symbol of the beauty of spiritual contemplation. If a man's spirit catches fire with love for the beauty of the Divinity and the divine, then though many years must pass in difficult labors of piety for the acquisition of the complete joy of salvation, they will seem only a few days, because he loves that for which he labors.

This also explains how the Apostles, in the midst of persecutions, continued to preach the Gospel from one end of the earth to the other; how the martyrs rejoiced in their sufferings; how the ascetics found blessedness in a severe and destitute life in the wilderness—and none of them would desire to change their way of life for any other.

Third of all, the ardency of one's zeal for God can be especially useful to protect a person against all temptations from the flesh and the world, as well as from the spirits of evil and delusion. Spiritual mentors explain this phenomenon with a simple comparison. When a cauldron boils on a fire, then no insect or household animal dares approach it to steal the food intended for man. But when it is taken off the fire and cools down, then all manner of insects swarm near it and fall into it, and a brazen dog might approach it, defile it, or steal it. Similarly, when the soul of man boils with the fire of divine desire, the spiritual fire is at the same time energy for action and a shield for protection. But if the careless allows his fire to go out and his pious zeal to cool down, then many vain, evil, impure thoughts are born and swarm in from the domain of the sensual. They fall into the depth of the soul and defile it, and then a brazen passion may approach and steal from the soul that which was being prepared to please God.

What do you think, brothers? Is not ardency of spirit toward God a quality much to be desired? So it is in truth! And this thought we find in the words of our own Savior. *I came to send fire on the earth, and how I wish it were already kindled!* What sort of a fire is this, so desirable to the One who came to save mankind? Without a doubt, this is not a destroying fire, but a fire that gives

Luke 12:49

life — a fire of the Spirit descending into the earth of the heart, with which, according to the prophetic expression, *He will sit as a refiner and a purifier of silver; He will purify the sons of Levi, and purge them as gold and silver, that they may offer to the Lord an offering in righteousness.*

Malachi 3:3

This divine fire, by which Jesus Christ so desired to arouse the hearts of men, already burned in His own heart as a fountainhead, as we see evidently in the following words: *But I have a baptism to be baptized with"* (that is, the suffering on the Cross) "*and how distressed I am till it is accomplished!* What is this distress, if not that His heart was on fire with desire to suffer and die on the Cross, so that by this sacrifice, He might accomplish man's salvation?

Luke 12:50

After such discourse, is it not painful, dear brothers, to think that some so-called Christians have their hearts still cold, foreign to the life of God — hearts which are earth into which the fire of Christ has not yet descended? Is it not sad to notice that some work for the Lord only superficially with the eternal works of piety and virtue, as if forced to do so, without any spiritual ardor, without sincere and profound eagerness? Poor people! They understand that it would be too dangerous not to work for the Lord completely. However, by working without eagerness, they damage themselves twice over. They both add to the weight of their labor, and they never reap a harvest from that labor.

Some may say, "We would like to have an ardent spirit, but what can we do if it is not given to us?" To this, we answer that if the divine Savior in the days of His earthly life so desired to cast this divine fire into the heart of mankind, then do you think that He desires it less now? *Jesus Christ is the same yesterday, today, and forever.* In Him—today as always, for each and for all—is life and light for mankind, a light that always shines, a life that constantly gives life. *Come unto Him, and be enlightened.* Lay the earth of your heart before Him, and He will light it on fire with His life-giving flame. Do for Him that small bit that you are able to now,

Hebrews 13:8

Psalm 33:6

and He will accomplish within you all that His omnipotence and all-goodness is able to. Arouse your heart with the remembrance of the countless and constant benevolences of God the Creator and Provider, and with the contemplation of the limitless love of the Redeemer who, not content to be merely our benefactor, made Himself a sacrifice and nourishment for you. Preserve, as much as this is possible, your conscience undisturbed and at peace, and if it becomes distressed with sin, do not wait to purify and pacify it with repentance. Force yourself without sloth and without complaining to work for the Lord with fear, until it is given to you to work for Him with joy. Do not ascribe any successes in God's service to yourself, but ascribe everything to the good grace of God. Keep yourself sober through prayer and humility, constantly bowing before God like earth before the sun. God is faithful, who shines His visible sun both on the good and the evil, according to the promise of His grace. He will also shine in our hearts, and He will warm and arouse your spirit by His Spirit, that you will be *not lagging in diligence, fervent in spirit, serving the Lord.* Not only like faithful slaves—diligent, fervent— but as children—joyful, with love—so that you may have internal consolation and reach the promised eternal blessings. Amen.

Romans 12:11

5

On Poverty of Spirit (1824)

*"Blessed are you poor in spirit, for yours
is the kingdom of God." (Luke 6:20)*

This is the foundational teaching that our divine Teacher and Lord, Jesus Christ, offered on a certain "level place." On this day, He was surrounded by *a crowd of His disciples and a great multitude of people from all Judea and Jerusalem, and from the seacoast of Tyre and Sidon, who came to hear Him and be healed of their diseases.*

Luke 6:17-18

And we also stand with Him on this *level place,* for here we see even the great nobleman standing no higher than any other man. We see the poor commoner no lower than anyone else. All stand before God, who abides on high and takes care of the lowly. And here we see *a crowd of His disciples,* for all Christians are the disciples of Christ. This crowd came here to approach and, as much as possible, come into contact with the holiness and power of God, and through this to *be healed of their diseases,* whether spiritual or physical. I hope that you all came with the thought that you will hear and learn the teaching of Christ.

SERMON 5: ON POVERTY OF SPIRIT

Those of you who have long been disciples, perhaps even from birth—do not be ashamed if we offer you the foundational teachings of Christ. Rather, hear this teaching with increased attention, for it is high time that you fulfill this teaching in action. For if you remain ignorant of this introductory teaching, it is not merely shameful for you, but fatal.

Blessed are you poor in spirit, for yours is the kingdom of God.

Let us praise our beloved Teacher for this beginning of instruction! What if He had begun instructing the people about the kingdom of God by speaking to all without distinction, with the words He spoke to Nicodemus alone: *Most assuredly, I say to you, unless one is born again, he cannot see the kingdom of God?* Then, in addition to Nicodemus' own questions (*How can a man be born when he is old? Can he enter a second time into his mother's womb and be born?*), Christ would have heard a host of other questions that would have been impossible to answer for carnal men! Or, what if He had offered His unprepared disciples the teaching of the Cross, which they hardly understood even after years of preparation (*But they did not understand this saying, and it was hidden from them so that they did not perceive it.*)? How hard would it have been to listen to Him and to accept what the people heard! Now, being compassionate to the infirmities of His listeners, Christ doesn't begin with the exalted. He doesn't inspire fear with His teaching. First of all, he makes it attractive, attracting the heart with the sweet words of "blessedness and the kingdom of God."

John 3:3

John 3:4

Luke 9:45

Who does not seek blessedness, wherever and however he can? Who doesn't desire the kingdom of God? What sort of mad or senseless person can remain cold or inattentive when he is offered blessedness, when he is promised the kingdom of God? Look. Here is the way to blessedness. Here is the door to the kingdom of God. It is poverty of spirit.

Blessed are the poor in spirit, for theirs is the kingdom of God. Is it not true that it is possible to throw away the entire world in

Luke 6:20

order to acquire this poverty, which gives blessedness and the kingdom of God?

O Christian! Disciple of blessedness! Disciple of the kingdom of God! Is not your heart pierced at these first words of Christ's teaching? Is not your heart enlarged to fit inside all that is said? Does not your mind thirst to understand what is poverty of spirit? Does not your spirit awaken to that salvific anxiety for salvation that demands that you find out how to become one of these poor in spirit? Listen and learn.

Luke 6:20   *Blessed are you poor in spirit, for yours is the kingdom of God.*

Once again let us praise our all-wise Teacher that He has clothed the all-wise teaching in simplicity of language, so that what is hidden from the wise and the learned is revealed even to children. What is more mysterious than the blessedness that everyone seeks everywhere, but no one can find anywhere? What is more inscrutable than the kingdom of God, since everything of God is inscrutable? On the contrary, what is more familiar and simpler than poverty, which we find everywhere among us? And using this familiar concept, our inimitable Teacher explains the mystery of attaining blessedness and the kingdom of God. Look at the horrifying poverty you see in the world around you. Contemplate it, and you will come to know blessed poverty of spirit.

The poor man has nothing, and he seeks everything from others. That which is necessary for life, such as food, clothing, and a home, he asks of others as a mercy. This is poverty of spirit. If your spirit remembers the life in Paradise from which it was exiled together with Adam, it must run and fall before God to beg for a spiritual home in His Church. If it sorrows for the loss of the Edenic clothing of light that sin tore off, it must beg God for spiritual clothing in the grace of His Son Jesus Christ (for if we have been baptized in Him, we have "put on Christ"). If our spirit hungers for the food of Paradise from the tree of life, of which it has been deprived, it must seek spiritual food in every word proceeding from the mouth of God. Such a spirit feels itself extremely deprived of all good things and in danger of eternal death. If you have such a spiritual disposition, God, who is rich in mercy, will see and accept you as one of the poor in spirit. He will then give you all the good things you ask for, and through them will grant you the very kingdom of God.

The first labor of the poor in spirit is to admit that in us and in the world, there is no true spiritual good thing, and then to zealously ask for spiritual alms from the Giver and Provider of everything good. Humble prayer and prayerful humility define poverty of spirit.

The deprivation of Eden's spiritual good things is the common lot of all who live on this earth. Therefore, it would seem that everyone on earth, without exception, should be poor in spirit. Truly, if we reason thus, there is not a single human being who is rich in spirit. However—and this is the worst of all!—there are those who think they are rich, that is, there are those poor who pretend to be rich. They are, if I am allowed the expression, rich in pride, vanity, hypocrisy, ignorance, and blindness. Therefore, they do not have the salvific sense of poverty of spirit.

One of these has done a few good or generous deeds, and he thinks that he is rich in virtue. Another has been praised by others, and he is sure that he has already achieved perfection. Yet another has managed merely to hide his sins, and so he has no more need of virtues. Yet another has become so accustomed to satisfying every desire of his flesh that he nearly has no knowledge of the needs of the spirit. Through the abundance of his earthly riches he hides from himself his lack of spiritual riches. Through the pleasures of the flesh, he dulls his spiritual sense. If his home is expansive, his clothing adorned, and his body full or even satiated, he is more than content. He looks with scorn at people who speak to him of spiritual hunger, of spiritual nakedness, of our calamitous state of exile from the uncreated and imperishable home of our heavenly Father, just as a rich man scorns the poor.

He who has an ear, let him hear what the Spirit says concerning this. *You say, 'I am rich, have become wealthy, and have need of nothing,'—and do not know that you are wretched, miserable, poor, blind, and naked.* Let us also hear what a fate is given by God to such who falsely imagine themselves to be rich. *He has filled the hungry with good things, and the rich He has sent empty away.* How can it be otherwise? Whoever thinks he is rich feels no want. Whoever feels no want will not ask for anything. Whoever will not ask, will receive nothing, as the Apostle James said, *You do not have because you do not ask.*

Our heavenly Provider is good. He tells us not to cast our pearls before swine, nor will He do likewise with his pearls. Furthermore, whoever does not ask for grace from God is not capable of accepting it, because his heart is closed. Therefore, it is also said, *Everyone who asks receives, and he who seeks finds, and to him who knocks it will be opened.*

O Christian! He who teaches us in the Gospel to be poor in spirit, *though He was rich, yet for your sakes He became poor, that you through His poverty might become rich.* If our obedience to Him, our gratitude, and our desire to partake in His promised, priceless kingdom requires us to cease being rich and become poor, then why are we sorry? Our inner, spiritual man will lose nothing if we have not already been enriched by the grace of Christ. To become poor in spirit merely means to know with conviction, and to admit with sincerity, that we were born, and abide, in spiritual poverty.

Can we be slothful concerning this? Can we be stubborn against this conviction? If it seems to you that you have acquired some virtue, "what do you have that you did not receive?" Was it not God who gave you the law of good, the light of your mind with which you saw this law, the sense in the heart with which you came to love this law, the witness of the conscience that did not allow you to reject or forget this law, and the power of will that moved you to fulfill this law? All these means for acquiring virtue are not your own. *Now if you did indeed receive it, why do you boast as if you had not received it?* 1 Corinthians 4:7

Make an account of and set aside everything in your acquired spiritual riches that you have received from God. Look. Do you have anything left, other than the poverty into which you were born? And what if the fruits of your righteousness have been damaged, like a worm, by impure motives and intentions? What if the few pennies that you've counted in your spiritual treasure house are counterbalanced by many thousands of pennies in debt, that is, in sins and falsehoods? Should you not, in this case, admit that you are the poorest of the poor? What if, instead of this admission, you drown out the sense of this poverty, putting all your trust in perishable earthly riches, or burdening your heart with overeating and drunkenness, or abandoning yourself to other sensual and bestial desires? Then you follow the path of the prodigal son, when he hungered and *would gladly have filled his stomach with the pods that the swine ate.* Luke 15:16

Let us acknowledge, we participants in the universal poverty, let us acknowledge, each in his own spirit, our poverty in spiritual good things, and let us humble ourselves. Let us admit our own sinfulness and repent. Let us often run to the home of our heavenly Father, asking Him for spiritual alms for the sake of Christ, His Only-begotten Son. For Christ became poor for our sakes, and He acquired the kingdom of grace for us by His blood. There is no doubt that if we ask, He will *give the Holy Spirit to those who ask Him* with faith, and this Comforter will teach us, through experience indescribable in words, how *blessed are the poor in spirit*, that truly theirs *is the kingdom of God.* Amen. Luke 11:13

Luke 6:20

6

On the Purification of the Heart (1826)

*"Blessed are the pure in heart,
for they shall see God." (Matthew 5:8)*

If you see an earthly king — and not just by accident, but because you are called into his presence — it is considered a great honor. How much greater must be the blessedness to see the heavenly King of kings and Lord of lords, whom you cannot see by accident, but only by His good will and grace! What do you see when you visit an earthly king? Glory, power, wisdom, goodness, and all this perhaps in great abundance, but still in limited form. What benefits come from such an audience? Wonder, love, hope, safety, and maybe a certain communion with kingly glory, though in a limited fashion.

But what do you see when you see God? Goodness and good itself, all-perfect and exclusive; wisdom and the very subject of wisdom; exalted and all-encompassing truth; limitless power and the power of powers; glory and beauty that no word can describe, that no imagination can conjure up. And what are the fruits of this contemplation? Not only the exaltation of wonder, the ecstasy of love, the fulfillment of all hopes, and safety untroubled by any evil, which cannot approach the gracious presence of God. What you receive is actual communion with the fullness of the One contemplated. For, according to Apostle Paul, *"We all, with unveiled face, beholding as in a mirror the glory of the Lord, are being transformed into the same image from glory to glory.*" 2 Corinthians 3:18

Do any of you desire to see God and to feel the blessedness of this contemplation? Then enter the path that leads to it. This path is indicated by Jesus Christ, who is Himself *the Way* and the most trustworthy Guide. This path is the purity or purification of the heart. *Blessed are the pure in heart, for they shall see God.* John 14:6 Matthew 5:8

Impurity of heart is more or less understandable to all, for everyone has experienced it, unfortunately, sometimes quite obviously. *For out of the heart proceed evil thoughts, murders, adulteries, fornications, thefts, false witness, blasphemies. These are the things which defile a man.* If evil thoughts proceeding from the heart visibly defile a man—whether he blasphemes against God or slanders his neighbor, or whether he robs, fornicates, commits adultery or murder—then who will not recognize an impure heart in these vile deeds or words? This makes it obvious that when a person begins the process of his heart's purification, he must reject all deeds that defile a man, that is, all sinful and unlawful actions. Without this, there is no hope not only of seeing the face God, but even of the smallest participation in the kingdom of God. *Do you not know that the unrighteous will not inherit the kingdom of God? Do not be deceived.* Do not delude yourself with any false hope that does not agree with this incontestable truth. Matthew 15:19-20 1 Corinthians 6:9

But here is something that some either do not notice or do not want to notice: even the heart of someone who does not defile himself with evil deeds and lawlessness is often impure. Let us repeat the words of the Knower of hearts: *For out of the heart proceed evil thoughts, murders, adulteries, fornications, thefts, false witness, blasphemies. These are the things which defile a man.* Notice how He reveals, in a single image, not only visible impurity, but invisible impurity as well? When evil thoughts come out of a heart and become actions, then they defile the whole man, both the inner Matthew 15:19-20 and outer man, both his heart and his members, both his soul and his body. But what about when evil thoughts do not come out of the heart to become actions, but remain nesting within the heart? What then?

Evidently, in this case, they defile the heart, the inner man, the soul. This internal impurity could be unnoticeable to others, as though it were nothing, when people only look at the face and actions of a man. However, for God, who sees the heart of man, this inner impurity is no less obvious or abhorrent than the external impurity of deeds. Therefore, the Lord categorizes evil thoughts as equally repugnant to evil deeds: *evil thoughts, murders, adulteries, fornications, thefts, false witness, blasphemies.*

Matthew 15:19

Perhaps you have not killed anyone, but have you desired in your heart that he would die? Listen. The Lord calls this evil thought murder. Your mouth has not opened to utter blasphemy against God. But has your heart been moved by brazen and ungrateful thoughts concerning God's judgments? Be careful! It is likely that the Knower of hearts has already heard your blasphemy. From this, it becomes obvious that actual purification of the heart, which makes man capable of seeing God, must be accomplished not only by rejection of all evil and lawless deeds, but also the rejection of every evil thought, for in each such thought an evil deed is concealed, like an embryo or seed.

How severe! This is the complaint of those who have no desire whatsoever to begin the labor of inner purification. How difficult! This is the complaint of those who have begun to attempt this labor.

Whether this requirement to reject all evil thoughts is severe or not, it is not we who have invented this requirement. It is not we who have made this a condition of seeing God and tasting the sweetness of divine blessedness. Rather, it is Christ who said, *Blessed are the pure in heart, for they shall see God.* You do not desire to subject yourself to this severity? Very well. But blame no one but yourself if you acquire no grace. However, is this require-

Matthew 5:8

ment for purity of heart truly that severe? Is the doctor who requires a painful surgery of the eyes cruel to the man who has lost his vision, if by this procedure, he promises a return to pure and complete vision? The evil thoughts that man does not reject (because he has become passionately attached to them) are like a cataract that dims spiritual vision to such a degree that man cannot see the light of natural truth even when he is close to it.

For example, he who is darkened by an angry thought cannot see the light of truth, becoming unable to distinguish between fault and innocence. He who is overwhelmed by the passion of sensuality cannot see the light of chastity, which is pleasant to the eyes both of men and God. He cannot even see that he ruins his own health. Is it any wonder, then, that the supernatural light of divinity is not accessible to such souls? And so, is it severity, or is it mercy that God does not want them to remain in the darkness that they have chosen, but rather He wants them, through inner purification, not only to return to the natural spiritual light of wisdom and virtue, but also to raise them up to the divine light of eternal truth and eternal blessedness?

As for the labor that accompanies this inner purification, I do not argue that it is heavy. If someone were to call it impossibly difficult, I would not argue either. However, the difficulty is lessened and the impossibility removed as soon as we apply our faith to the words of the Word who created everything out of nothing: *The things which are impossible with men are possible with God, all things are possible to him who believes.* *Mark 9:23 Luke 18:27*

With the help of the grace of God, it is not difficult to come to hate evil thoughts, which are truly hateful and revolting to the man who has not yet lost the natural faculties of his conscience. It is not difficult to reject that which is hateful. After decisively rejecting these evil thoughts, it is not difficult to cast these thoughts out of the heart through the power of good thoughts, prayers, the fear of God, and the name of the Lord Jesus, which is especially powerful at destroying all evil. If they return, or if we encounter them by accident, against our own will, then they will either not have the power to defile the heart that has rejected them, or they will cast a temporary shadow on the heart, which will disappear with a humble thought or through the sorrow of repentance.

Let us not be lazy, brothers, and let us not fear labor. Let us stand fast in our asceticism, *let us cleanse ourselves from all filthiness of flesh and spirit.* Even more so, He will *create in [us] a clean heart* by His grace. No matter how great or prolonged the labor of the purification of our heart, O God, may Thou find us worthy at the end, through this purification, of seeing Thy glory in Thy kingdom. Amen.

2 Corinthians 7:1
Psalm 50:12

7

On Consecrating the Day of the Lord (1849)

"And Jesus, answering, spoke to the lawyers and Pharisees, saying, 'Is it lawful to heal on the Sabbath?'" (Luke 14:3)

On one occasion, the Lord Jesus, looking with the eye of His omniscience on the hidden thoughts of the lawyers and Pharisees, called them out into the open with the question: *Is it lawful to heal on the Sabbath?* Is it permissible to heal the sick on a day that is consecrated to God? The lawyers, who were supposed to know the law, found no answer. *But they kept silent.* In this silence was hidden a strict opinion that healing others is not allowed on a Sabbath, as well as a desire to accuse Jesus for His healing on the Sabbath, so that they could condemn Him of being a law-breaker. However, the strict judges did not dare to open their mouths, because the people revered Jesus and were astounded by His healing.

Therefore, the Lord of the Sabbath answered His own question. And...how easy and indisputable was His answer, even for those who opposed Him! He immediately healed a man who stood before His eyes, suffering of dropsy. *And He took him and*

Luke 14:3

Luke 14:4

healed him, and let him go. Obviously, the healing was miraculous. The work of miracles is the work of God. The work of God cannot be contrary to the law of God. Consequently, healing the sick on a day consecrated to God is not contrary to the law of God. *It is lawful to heal on the Sabbath.*

It is known to you that Sunday holds the same significance in the Christian Church as the Sabbath did in the Old Testament.

A question: is it permissible for a doctor to treat his patient on a Sunday? I don't think any of you—educated or uneducated—would hesitate with your answer. Who would fail to send for a doctor on a Sunday? What physician would refuse to visit his sick patient on a Sunday? So why do we answer thus, while the Jews answered in the opposite way? Is it because we understand the Law of God better than the Jews? If that is so, well and good. However, can it be perhaps, on the contrary, that we are less attentive to the Law of the Sabbath than the Jews? Clearly, that would be humiliating for us Christians.

Thus, it is necessary for us, brother Christians, to think and take care to know and fulfill the Law of the day of the Lord, not only no worse than the ancient Hebrews did, but in a more perfect way, since Christianity, without a doubt, is greater and more perfect than Judaism.

Let us be guided by the Law and the Old Testament.

What is the substance of the original law of the Sabbath, that is, the law concerning the day of rest, the day of the Lord? *Remember the Sabbath day, to keep it holy...The seventh day is the Sabbath of the Lord your God. In it you shall do no work.* Take note. The day is completely consecrated to the Lord. Not a single portion of that day is allotted for man and his work. It would also be useful to note that the day is measured in the same way as it was from the beginning, during the creation of the world, as we read in Genesis: *So the evening and the morning were the first day.* Therefore, as before in the Hebrew, and now in the Christian Church, which is always faithful to ancient traditions, the feast always began and begins on the evening of the day before the feast, and finishes during the evening of the feast day, as you see in the order of services.

Perhaps some will complain that it is impossible to dedicate an entire 24-hour period to God, since people need at least part of every day for themselves. For example, people need time to dress, time to eat, and to fortify the body with necessary sleep. This objection is resolved, first of all, by the fact that a person can labor to deny himself in some of his necessities to avoid stealing time dedicated to God. Secondly, even daily activities can be done for God, and thereby can be sanctified and put in accordance with the law of the Sabbath. For example, one can dress on the day of the Lord with the pious thought that clean clothes can symbolize the cleanliness and holiness of the day and the temple of God which should be attended on this day. This is the correct use of festal clothing, which fallen custom has perverted in our times into a kind of idol worship of vanity and self-love. Or, according to the words of Ezra, *Eat the fat, drink the sweet,* but *whether you eat or drink...do all to the glory of God,* with joy and a heart grateful to God. This is a good principle for any festal meal, which in ancient times in some ways was connected to sacrifice and divine service. The thought that even the night of a feast is part of the day of the Lord can and should inspire a person to sanctify this portion, as much as possible, with God-pleasing asceticism. You should give as little time as possible to the inactivity of sleep. This is the beginning of all-night vigils, which need, weakness, and self-will have all partially shortened to such a degree that the name "All-night Vigil" has become an accusation of deteriorated zeal in the labor of prayer.

Nehemiah 8:10
1 Corinthians 10:31

What else does the ancient law of the Sabbath declare? *You shall keep the Sabbath, therefore, for it is holy to you. Everyone who profanes it shall surely be put to death; for whoever does any work on it, that person shall be cut off from among his people.*

Exodus 31:14

What else does Holy Scripture say about this subject? Once, while wandering through the desert, the Israelites *found a man gathering sticks on the Sabbath day*. I do not know if we would hesitate to determine the severity of the crime, but then, the entire congregation, including Moses and Aaron, did not know what to do with him: "It had not been explained what should be done to him." But ultimately *the congregation brought him outside the camp and stoned him with stones, and he died.*

In the book of the Prophet Jeremiah, we read of a terrible threat of wrath from the face of God for any lawbreaking against the Sabbath, even examples that may seem not very serious: *But if you will not heed Me to hallow the Sabbath day, such as not carrying a burden when entering the gates of Jerusalem on the Sabbath day, then I will kindle a fire in its gates, and it shall devour the palaces of Jerusalem, and it shall not be quenched.* We know with what terrifying exactness did this threat become reality through the Babylonians.

We cannot fail to remind you of yet another example of willing strictness in keeping the holiness of the day of the Lord: the Maccabean brothers. Many Hebrews fled into the desert during the time of Antiochus' persecutions and attempts to force them into paganism. The pagans understood that it would be a good idea to attack them on a Sabbath, because according to the law, they were supposed to be at rest. Then, zealots of piety were faced suddenly with a question never before considered: was it permissible to go into battle on the Sabbath? And what do you think was their answer? *Let us all die in our innocence*, they said, and nearly one thousand people allowed themselves to be slaughtered, refusing to defend themselves in any way. This circumstance, however, made it clear to the Maccabees that the pagans would successfully exterminate piety from among the Jews if they continued thus. Therefore, it was accepted as a rule: to battle on a Sabbath was permissible.

After what we have said already, let anyone who desires still wonder at the strictness of the ancient law concerning the day of the Lord. For my part, I am more astounded by the law's importance and power. Let others condemn the extremism of some zealots of the Lord's day, but is not their reverence before the law and their self-sacrifice for the sake of the law more worthy of respect? Go ahead and boast in the superiority of the Christian understanding of the law over the Hebrew, but have a care to prove yourselves worthy of such boasting. The most convincing proof of an exalted understanding of the law is exalted asceticism and virtue.

Or do you perhaps think that a more exalted understanding of the law of the Sabbath requires less of you or even allows you more indulgence, in accordance with the new freedom of grace, contrary to the slavery of the Old Testament? Let us see what the Gospel says about this question.

What man is there among you who has one sheep, and if it falls into a pit on a Sabbath, will not lay hold of it and lift it out? Of how much more value then is man than a sheep? Therefore it is lawful to do good on the Sabbath. The Sabbath was made for man, and not man for the Sabbath. Therefore the Son of Man is also Lord of the Sabbath. We can extrapolate two rules from these citations. First: It is permissible to do work on the Sabbath if it is absolutely necessary. Second: Good deeds and deeds of love for others are worthy of the day of the Lord. However, the opposite is also true. We have no recourse but to admit that any work that is not absolutely necessary, or any work that does not have special moral significance, remains forbidden on the day of the Lord, both by word of the Gospel and the law of Moses.

Matthew 12:11-12
Mark 2:27-28

As for the majestic declaration of the Lord—"The Son of Man is also Lord of the Sabbath"—hearing this, do not think that the Lord, who created the Sabbath, did Himself break the law of the Sabbath or allow others to do so. He said that he did not come to destroy the law, but to fulfill it (see Matthew 5:17). And having called Himself "the Lord of the Sabbath," He revealed His divinity and authority to correctly interpret the law of the Sabbath (for who can better interpret a law than the Giver of the law Himself?), fulfill it, and renew it. He especially showed this authority in that He, while preserving the essence of the original law to dedicate the seventh day to the Lord, also sanctified for it a new day by His glorious resurrection. The ancient Sabbath day, celebrated in remembrance of the creation of the world, was never completely joyful from the moment that the created was stricken with sin. Therefore, it was right and just that it would give way to the new Sabbath day of the resurrection, in honor of the day of the new creation, by which we are *created in Christ Jesus for good works, begotten...again to a living hope through the resurrection of Jesus Christ from the dead.* Do you see how the Lord of the Sabbath did not destroy it, but made it even more important? Therefore, if the ancient day of the Lord was honored as holy and worthy of reverence—a day of rest in honor of the first, temporary creation—then should the new Sabbath not be honored as even more holy and worthy of reverence, since it is the day of resurrection, the day of joy for the new creation that will abide for all ages?

Ephesians 2:10
1 Peter 1:3

Brothers! The question of the Lord—*Is it lawful to heal on the Sabbath?*—remained without an answer. This shows us that the truth gives us wisdom not only by reasoning through and answering a question, but by the question being asked in and of itself, for in some cases there is only one possible answer, found in the conscience of the listener. Let us follow the steps of our heavenly Teacher, and let us ask our own consciences some questions, whose answers, I believe, are already prepared by the arguments I have offered you today.

Luke 14:3

Is it worthy for Christians, the children of the freedom of grace, to care less about keeping the Lord's day than the slaves of the law, merely because today we are not threatened by a death by stoning?

Is it proper not to go to God's temple on the morning of Sunday, the holy day itself, and instead, choose to go to the market, having the day overflow with bustling about in the midst of the

SERMON 7: ON CONSECRATING THE DAY OF THE LORD

crowds, buying and selling, instead of praying in a state of calmness? The civic law is lenient in its permission to keep markets open on Sundays, but only to buy and sell what is absolutely necessary for the day. It would be better if we only used this leniency in cases of necessity, and even so--the less, the better. But if we buy and sell things that we could put off to a work day, if we sell it only for the sake of avarice, or if we buy it only because it's easier on a day of rest, then is this worthy behavior? Are six days of the week not enough for such buying and selling? Is it worth it to barge into the seventh day, so that we place a stamp of sin against the commandment sanctifying the seventh day on all that we have bought and sold?

On the eve of the Lord's day, during the hours that belong, as we have explained already, to the consecrated portion of the Sabbath, the Church already begins its triumphant doxologies. For our pious ancestors, it was normal to partake of spiritual joy during the evening service or the vigil. Is it worthy of their descendants to hurry to various places of worldly diversion, to plays that should not command the attention of any Christian, especially at such important times, since they have come down to us from the pagans, and they hardly ever rise above pagan conceptions of vanity, passions, and vices?

Is it worthy of us, on the day consecrated to the glory of Christ the Savior and the joy of salvation, to indulge in works, masquerading as amusements, that not only do not glorify God, but debase man and harm his salvation? For these are the works of licentiousness, immoderation, and excess.

He who has ears to hear, let him hear. That is, whoever has a conscience that still speaks to him, let him listen how it answers the questions I have offered. *Matthew 11:15*

May the commandments, the Church, and our consciences direct our actions always, but especially on the holy day of the Lord! As for the freedom that you have received on the feast day? Use it to avoid slavery to your passions, vain customs, and condemnation of examples worthy of emulation. Amen.

8

On Blessed Childbearing (1828)

"And I will bless her and also give you a son by her; then I will bless her, and she shall be a mother of nations; kings of peoples shall be from her." (Genesis 17:16)

How happy are Abraham and Sarah! For a long time, they had no children. But now, they will have a child, and even before the birth, they know that it will be blessed.

Who among you who desire to become parents, or have already become parents, does not also desire to have good and blessed children? But since not all children correspond to the desires of their parents, then a natural question arises: How does one raise good and blessed children?

After all, good children do not always come from good parents, but sometimes from evil ones. The opposite is also true—sometimes good parents have evil children. Or at least so say the spectators of the superficial. They explain it by saying that "It just happens." I would ask such people to interpret this mysterious phrase: "It just happens." When wheat grows in a field where it has been sown, you do not say, "It just happens." Rather, when you see a stalk of wheat growing in a meadow where it was not sown, then you say, "It just happens." What are you trying to say with these words? Doubtless, you are not saying that the stalk of wheat grew from no seed, or that the seed somehow spontaneously generated in the ground, or something equally foolish. On the contrary, you must mean that you do not know how the seed was carried to this place—whether by the wind or dropped by a casual passer-by. Therefore, the phrase, "It just happens," is nothing more than an attempt to avoid the resolution of a difficult question or an acceptable method to gracefully conceal your ignorance without shame.

Consequently, the idea that chance determines whether parents raise good or evil children—"It just happens!"—is a thought that can bring conscientious parents to despair. It would even be an expression of a kind of unfairness of fate against them. Thank goodness, such an idea is unfounded and completely worthless. These are words that express no more than a lack of any ideas that are capable of explaining this phenomenon.

So where do good children come from? We would not need to search long for a general rule if we saw all good and wise parents, who took care for the upbringing of their children, produce equally good children. The question is resolved if we say that it is just as natural as when a field sowed with wheat produces a harvest of wheat, not weeds.

Do not all doctors admit it as incontrovertible that some diseases are passed on from the parents to the children? It is even less subject to scrutiny to suggest that the health of the parents is also a genetic gift to their children, if unusual circumstances do not steal this natural inheritance from them. Also, when we look at children's faces, do we not notice similarity to their parents? Thus, if we find that the parents are themselves responsible for certain physical perfections or imperfections of their children, then what prevents us from saying the same concerning the more exalted qualities of the spirit, such as spiritual dispositions and inclinations?

Perhaps some will ask, "How can something spiritual be passed on from the parents to the children through birth when the soul is a simple substance, which cannot be divided to pass on part of itself to another soul?" To this I answer, first of all, that the passing on of certain moral inclinations and good disposition from the parents to the children happens not only through birth but also thanks to a wise upbringing. Secondly, I will ask a question of my own. How can something physical pass on from parent to child when their bodies are formed anew from formless matter taken from the bodies of the parents? How can the new body then be directed by its own personal soul, constantly developing thanks to the intake of food and the exit of waste materials? But our ignorance concerning these processes does not deny our experience that this truly does occur. I will even dare to say more. Is it not naturally easier to accept it as fact when we find something inherited from the parents in the child's soul? After all, the soul is a simple substance, and it reveals all its capabilities and powers within itself, from its inner source of existence received at birth. On the contrary, the body's development depends on so many external factors of nature!

However, lest we think that the truth depends on "the thoughts of men," which are all, without exception, *but vain* compared to the knowledge of God, I call you to stand before the judgment of this eternally-unchanging knowledge of God, and I ask you this: To whom is given the blessing of God - *Be fruitful and multiply*? Is it given to the body of man, which without a soul would never understand this blessing and would never be able to fulfill it? Or is it given to the whole man, and especially to his soul? Do these words of the Scripture refer to the body: *So God created man in His own image; in the image of God He created him; male and female He created them*? God has no body; consequently, man is created according to the image and likeness of God in his soul. After this, I ask another question, and we will understand much from its answer.

Psalm 93:11

Genesis 1:28

Genesis 1:27

SERMON 8: ON BLESSED CHILDBEARING

What do these words about Adam mean: *Adam...begot a son in his own likeness, after his image, and named him Seth?* Does this mean that Seth looked like his father in his facial features and the build of his body? Would it be worth even mentioning such a trivial and short detail in such a holy narrative? And does not the obvious parallel between Adam's image and God's image indicate to us that the writer of Genesis spoke about the inner image, the spiritual and moral one? The command to create—*be fruitful and multiply*—implanted in Adam the capability of giving birth to blessed children and passing on to them the image of God as their inheritance, for he himself was created in this image. However, when Adam's sin perverted the image of God in him, then—even though, through the power of the original creative command, he was able to produce a son—he was no longer able to produce anything other than what he had within himself. *He begot a son* not in the full and complete image of God, as he himself was created, but *in his own likeness, after his own image*. In other words, what Adam passed on to his son had certain remnants of the image of God, but intermixed with sin and his own spiritual damage.

These are the original divine and the subsequent natural laws that govern human birth. Being written in the Book of Genesis after the birth of Seth, it can never be erased. And so, it is natural that all parents give birth to children in their own likenesses, after their own images. Sinners give birth to sinners, just as sickly parents give birth to sickly children. However, this also means that the grace of God helps parents who have freely labored in repentance, prayer, and good deeds—thereby weakening their sinful inclinations and strengthening their good intentions—by giving their children a certain natural inclination toward good and special help against the power of sin (even though it must be said that in all cases sin is defeated by free will and especially with the help of grace).

Genesis 5:3

Genesis 1:28

Genesis 5:3
Genesis 5:3

We see an early indication of this spiritual and natural law in the story of the wife of Manoah. An angel appeared to her and foretold that she, being up to this moment barren, would give birth to a son, and that *the child shall be a Nazirite to God from the womb*. At the same moment, he commanded that she, from that moment, begin a life of temperance proper to the Nazirites, even during her pregnancy: *She may not eat anything that comes from the vine, nor may she drink wine or similar drink, nor eat anything unclean.* It is almost the same thing as if he said, "Your son must be a Nazirite; however, to make this eventuality more certain, you must prepare him for such a way of life even while you bear him in your womb. Lead the life of a Nazirite; and in this manner, you will prepare him for a capability and an inclination for the Nazirite way of life."

Judges 8:3-5

Judges 13:14

In order to make this general law of birth accord with certain situations that, it would seem, are an exception to the rule and even seem to contradict it—such as when good parents give birth to unworthy children, or when good children come from unworthy parents, or when brilliant children come from unremarkable parents—we must remember that God is just as much an all-powerful and unchangeable Lawgiver to the world in His judgments as He is an all-wise and free Ruler of that world. He is the all-righteous Judge not only of visible deeds, but of the hidden dispositions of every person. To avoid long discourses on this subject, let us use some vivid examples.

Even Adam gave birth to diametrically opposed sons—Cain, Abel, and Seth! Where is the one common law governing birth here? Be attentive and observe. Adam, freshly (so to speak) poisoned by his recently committed sin, placed himself in the position of a kind of badly-thought-out brazenness of hope, because of God's promise of eventual redemption. In this spiritual state, he gave birth to Cain, who was a brazen sinner. Then Adam, having experienced the heaviness of the curse in the unhappy birth of Cain, was still attracted to sin, still deluded by his hope, and humiliated by vanity. In this state, he gave birth to Abel, who was meek, but unstable. Finally, Adam deepened himself into humility by the continuation of his sorrows. Being confirmed in his hope by his endurance, and being confirmed in his endurance by his hope, he gave birth to Seth, the trustworthy foundation of his posterity.

Abraham also gave birth to two different sons. Ishmael was like a "wild ass," as the prophecy said concerning him, while Isaac was the blessing of all nations. What led to such a difference? The slave girl Hagar's passionate nature obstructed the blessing of Abraham in his son Ishmael, but the virtuous and humble Sarah combined the blessing of Abraham on Isaac with her own blessing, born of her purity and virtue. As God said concerning her, *And I will bless her and also give you a son by her; then I will bless her, and she shall be a mother of nations; kings of people shall be from her.* *Genesis 17:16*

Even stranger is the birth, from Isaac and Rebecca, of such diametrically opposed twins as Esau and Jacob. What can we say to explain such an unusual phenomenon? Only that which God himself said to Rebecca: *Two nations are in your womb.* Two opposite principles acted at the same time in her womb—the inherited sin of Adam and the blessing of God. The first expressed itself strongly in Esau, whereas the second gained the upper hand in Jacob. *Genesis 25:23*

Let us take one more example from the history of the kings of the Jews. The son of the idol-worshiper Ahaz was the pious Hezekiah, but Manasseh, the son of Hezekiah, was also an idol-worshiper, though he later repented. These vagaries could perhaps be easily explained if we had enough information about the manner of these kings' upbringing. For the fate of the children of famous and rich people often depends a great deal on their teachers and mentors. Good instructors can become positive tools of Providence, while evil teachers are instruments wielded in the hands of God for the punishment of the sins of the parents and for their lack of care in upbringing. However, we must also consider that God's blessings and punishments in families do not always exactly follow the virtues or vices of every person in the family. Sometimes they come quickly to cut off evil and strengthen good in humanity at large, and sometimes they lag, to give room for endurance and long-suffering or to save the blessings, so to speak, for a time when they are more needed.

The Lord Himself says this of Himself: *The Lord, the Lord God, merciful and gracious, longsuffering, and abounding in goodness and truth, keeping mercy for thousands of generations, forgiving iniquity and transgression and sin, by no means clearing the guilty, visiting the iniquity of the fathers upon the children and the children's children to the third and the fourth generation.* If someone were to complain about this cruelty of *visiting the iniquity of the fathers upon the children...to the third and the fourth generation*, the all-good God amply justifies His judgments by His "mercy," which He does not visit only on four generations, but on "thousands" of them.

It seems to me that these contemplations and examples prove that marriage and the calling of parenthood are not such things that can be left as victims to the passions and as playthings for frivolity—not without punishment. Those who wish to have worthy children will act wisely if they make themselves worthy parents first of all. Amen.

Exodus 34:6-7

9

On Love of Work (1847)

"But in all things we commend ourselves as ministers of God: in much patience, in tribulations, in needs, in distresses, in stripes, in imprisonments, in tumults, in labors..." (2 Corinthians 6:4-5)

St. Paul, as the planter of the church in Corinth, wrote to the Corinthians specifically. Also, as the Apostle to the nations, he writes to all Christians: *We then, as workers together with Him also plead with you not to receive the grace of God in vain.* In other words, he exhorts all Christians to live life in such a way that the grace of God, accepted by them from Christ through His sacraments, would not leave them fruitless, but that they would actively use grace's help to confirm their salvation through the doing of good deeds. Without becoming like the teachers who lay heavy and unbearable burdens on the shoulders of others (and themselves don't even lift them with their own fingers), the Apostle, on the contrary, shows himself to have borne, and to have continued bearing, heavy and even unbearable burdens, so that his disciples would not disdain lifting a burden less than they are capable of. *But in all things we commend ourselves as ministers of God: in much patience, in tribula-*

2 Corinthians 6:1

tions, in needs, in distresses, in stripes, in imprisonments, in tumults, in labors, and in many other kinds of ascetic labors and virtues, which I do not list in full for the sake of brevity.

From this multitude of burdens, truly heavy (more or less) for fallen nature, but not unbearable with the help of grace, I now lift up one. It is one of the most inescapable and easiest of burdens, and I desire also that others will bear the same burden on their shoulders. By this I refer specifically to *labors*. I pray you, with the Apostle, *We commend ourselves as ministers of God…in labors*.

Perhaps this teaching concerning labors is not worth the effort, or even unworthy of the bishop's cathedra? Will not some say that whoever needs to labor will go to that labor without instruction, unwillingly, or pushed by his passions? Why is it necessary to pointlessly torture those who can get by without laboring?

If anyone admits having such thoughts in his head, or, after careful self-examination, finds them in the disposition of his life, then let him accept my insistence that the presence of such thoughts makes the necessity of this teaching all the more evident and worthy of attention.

Is unwilling labor any better than the work of an ox who bears a yoke and pulls the plough? Is it not especially heavy, first of all because of the difficulty of the labor itself and, secondly, because of the oppressive sense of slavery? And therefore, would it not be good if we could raise up even the lowliest work of man above the work of irrational beasts? Would it not be good to replace the oppressive sense of slavery with the easy-to-bear burden of moral necessity, acknowledged by the mind?

To work because of the passions, for example, because of desire for monetary gain—is it noble? Is it not also combined with torture, because every predominant passion is an inner torturer? Therefore, would it not be better if we make our labors noble by casting out, or at the very least defeating, the humiliating

SERMON 9: ON LOVE OF WORK

tendency toward avarice with an exalted incitement to ascetic action?

Perhaps some would not agree to label labors inspired by ambition as ignoble. Without arguing with these, I would only ask the powerful and the exalted, "Are they completely content with their subordinates if they work only to acquire more exalted positions and honors? Would they not perhaps desire for their workers to be inspired by purer motives? Such as profound respect, fidelity, diligence, and love?

What can we say about disdain and abhorrence for labors and a life of idleness? If life is activity, then, on the contrary, idleness and laziness are not life, or at least not the life of a reasoning and moral creature. Sleeping in late in the morning, getting up slowly, then a long breakfast, a walk outside, idle talk with guests, or perhaps, which is no better, vapid reading, then lunch, a nap, some kind of play, card games, dinner, and again a long night's sleep—is this the life of a reasoning and moral creature?

Therefore, unwilling work, labors incited by passions, repulsion from work, and slothfulness—all this requires either correction or improvement through a healthy teaching concerning labors. And naturally, there is no better source for such a teaching than in the fountainhead of the Christian love of wisdom.

Is there work in heaven? We cannot say for certain; however, we do know from the Revelation of St. John that the Powers there *do not rest day or night*, singing constant doxologies to the Pantocrator. But there, it is not like here on earth. Here labors, rest, and pleasures are divided, demarcated, bisected. There, the activity of the created Powers does not require rest, and their labors, rest, and blessedness in God are all one and the same. However, I believe that the good spirits *sent forth to minister for those who will inherit salvation* do labor, and their labor is not easy. For they have to descend from the pure and bright domain of heaven into the shadowy and humid abyss of earth. They have to be vigilant in the face of our unworthiness. They send to us their subtle, spir-

Revelation 4:8

Hebrews 1:14

itual suggestions that are often drowned out by our sensuality. They have to endure all our shortcomings and unfaithfulness, and sometimes they have to depart from us because of our impurities, but not too far, so that once again they might catch the right moment for their beneficial approach. Finally, sometimes they sorrow without consolation when we do not repent.

Think of this seriously, son of dust! If the inhabitants of heaven do not consider themselves too exalted to come down from their blessed heaven to miserable earth in order to labor for the sake of your salvation, then how dare you reject any kind of beneficial work as though it were beneath you or unpleasant to you? You should only be on your guard against dishonorable thoughts, for they alone make any kind of labor truly dishonorable.

If we ask, "Was there labor in the garden of Eden?" The book of Genesis answers us, *Then the Lord God took the man and put him in the garden of Eden to tend and keep it.* Eden had no special need of man's cultivating hand, as our own gardens and fields do today, because the curse that gave rise to weeds and thistles had not yet been uttered. So what did man in Eden *tend and keep*? St. John Chrysostom answers this by offering the words of the Wise Man: *For idleness teaches much evil.* Therefore, he concludes, God "wanted him for a while to take some slight care that was appropriate in both watching and tilling. If, after all, he had been relieved of all need to work, he would have fallen victim to great indulgence and at once slipped into sloth; whereas, in fact, by performing some work that was painless and without difficulty he would be brought to a better frame of mind."[2] We must learn this explanation of the golden-mouthed teacher so that, even if any of us lives in nearly Edenic prosperity and abundance, even if nothing ever required us to work, we should still not disdain work or avoid it. Instead, we should use it as a guard over our inner and outer prosperity, lest idleness come to teach us much evil.

Genesis 2:15

Sirach 33:28

---

2   St. John Chrysostom, *Homilies on Genesis*.

However, our state is hardly paradisaical. And in our fallen state, work has a new meaning and is newly necessary. For pride and disobedience, God the Judge said to man, cast out of Eden, *In the sweat of your face you shall eat bread.* In other words, as St. John Chrysostom explains, "Since, however, such indulgence was of no benefit to you, accordingly I curse the ground so that it will not in the future yield its harvest as before without tilling and ploughing; instead, I invest you with great labor, toil and difficulty, and with unremitting pain and despair, and I am ensuring that everything you do is achieved only by sweat, so that under pressure from these, you may have continual guidance in keeping to limits and recognizing your own makeup."[3]

Genesis 3:19

If work thus is the universal punishment from God to man, and at the same time God's instruction toward humility and self-knowledge of weakness that must always lead to the mollification of God the Judge, then can it be possible to avoid work, the just punishment of God, without the danger of an even greater punishment? Is it not mad to run away from work, since it is the instruction given by God? Should we not fear the conviction of a new judgment of God, which will sound like this: "Since you knew that for inattentive labor and slothfulness man in Eden was brought down from painless toil to painful labors on the earth (though they be beneficial), but still you did not want to take advantage of this salvific remedy, then all I have left to do is to bring you to an even lower level—to tortuous and fruitless labor in the abyss"?

It must be said that Christianity, which makes everything easier, better, sweeter, and more perfect, prescribes work for us, but not so much as a punishment of God as a form of service to God: *But in all things we commend ourselves as ministers* [i.e. servants] *of God, by the way, in labors as well.* In what way? If work is necessary, then consider it not blind necessity, but the providence of

2 Corinthians 6:4-5

---

3   Ibid.

God's wisdom in human life. Therefore, bear it not with a feeling of slavery, but with a sense of obedience to the will of God. And if, because of social mores, another person forces you to work for him, then bear that burden not only for the sake of your superior, but for God as well, *not with eyeservice, as men-pleasers, but as bondservants of Christ, doing the will of God from the heart.* If you are burdened by others with heavy and prolonged labors, then offer your work as a sacrifice of endurance and your lack of complaining to God. If nothing forces you to work, then it should be even easier for you to imagine yourself the servant of God in the work that you will undertake for the good of your neighbor. After all, service for the sake of your neighbor's benefit is true service to Christ, as He Himself said, *Assuredly, I say to you, inasmuch as you did it to one of the least of these My brethren, you did it to Me.*

Ephesians 6:6

Matthew 25:40

I will say one more definitive apostolic word concerning work. Will I direct it especially to the noble-born, the free, and the rich, or will I refrain, lest they send me to join the slaves and manual laborers? But the apostolic word speaks to all, and since he speaks, I have no right to remain silent, no matter how important my audience. What is this word? *We commanded you this: If anyone will not work, neither shall he eat.* As we extend our hand, untouched by labors, to partake of our extensive table, we should consider whether we are worthy, according to this testament or command, to share bread and water with this tent-maker, who, having taught others to work, required even more from himself in his apostolic duties and in common manual labor.

2 Thessalonians 3:10

In his own words: *Yes, you yourselves know that these hands have provided for my necessities, and for those who were with me;* "*and we labor, working with our own hands; nor did we eat anyone's bread free of charge, but worked with labor and toil night and day, that we might not be a burden to any of you.* But whoever is not worthy to eat with Paul will of course be also unworthy to eat with Christ at His table in His kingdom.

Acts 20:34
1 Corinthians 4:12

2 Thessalonians 3:8

Let us not be lazy, idle, and slothful. Let us come to love work. Let us do what is beneficial, even if it is because we need to, but also because we love our neighbor. Then, because of our virtue, according to the promise of the Apostle, we not only will eat earthly food with a peaceful conscience, but, finally, we will also partake of the immortal feast. As Christ the Lord Himself promised us, *And I bestow upon you a kingdom, just as My Father bestowed one upon Me, that you may eat and drink at My table in My kingdom.* Amen.

Luke 22:29-30

10

On Works of Mercy (1848)

"And I say to you, make friends for yourselves by unrighteous mammon, that when you fail, they may receive you into an everlasting home." (Luke 16:9)

Is not almsgiving spoken of too much? Can we possibly say any more?

Whoever loves almsgiving will not find my words tedious, because people do not grow tired of hearing about subjects that they love. If anyone is not disposed to listen often to speeches about almsgiving, he can truly ask himself whether or not he loves almsgiving enough. In such cases, it is not excessive to speak once again about almsgiving.

How rich has the world become in calamities and sorrows! It is necessary that the children of God should grow no less rich in their works of mercy and almsgiving.

Whoever wants to become rich thinks often of different paths to gaining money. Similarly, whoever wants to become rich in works of mercy also must often think of the different ways of acquiring this imperishable treasure that cannot be stolen.

The Gospel confirms us in this thought. It is well known how many different subjects would have fit in the Gospel, if only there was enough room to fit them in. As the Evangelist said, *There are also many other things that Jesus did, which if they were written one by one, I suppose that even the world itself could not contain the books that would be written.* Therefore, one may think that perhaps not many citations will be found in the Gospel about almsgiving, since it is apparently such a simple and everyday matter. However, the Gospel, or rather Christ the Savior Himself, spoke often and in different ways about almsgiving. This, without a doubt, corresponds to the importance of the subject.

John 21:25

Christ sees people who are only starting to seek the path to salvation and blessedness. Taking advantage of their early enthusiasm for salvation and blessedness, He sows seeds of mercy in this rich soil: *Blessed are the merciful, for they shall obtain mercy.*

Matthew 5:7

He sees souls already capable of more exalted states, and, in order to teach them mercy and non-acquisitiveness, and generous almsgiving that extends even to enemies, He shows them the most exalted model for emulation: *Therefore be merciful, just as your Father is also merciful. For He makes His sun rise on the evil and on the good, and sends rain on the just and on the unjust.*

Luke 6:36
Matthew 5:45

He enters the home of a man who loves hospitality, and He transforms the meal into an occasion for instruction in mercy. *But when you give a feast, invite the poor, the maimed, the lame, the blind. And you will be blessed, because they cannot repay you; for you shall be repaid at the resurrection of the just."*

Luke 14:13-14

He sees people who have no time to think of the works of mercy, because their time is too taken up with active idleness and idle activity related to the strict fulfillment of the laws of contemporary fashion in clothing and interior design, feasting, and parties. The more they are active in this sensual life, the deeper they fall asleep spiritually. A very strong medicine is needed to wake them up. This medicine is a parable in which Christ shows them a mirror of the present and the future: *There was a certain rich man who was clothed in purple and fine linen and fared sumptuously every day...* Therefore, he had no time to even notice that the poor and afflicted Lazarus lay at his very gates. Here is the present! And here is the future! The merciless rich man, in hellish tortures of fire, cannot even reach for a drop of water to cool the tongue that had enjoyed such refined food and drink during life.

Luke 16:19

The heavenly Teacher sees the lawyer who does not reject the commandment to love his neighbor, but who tries to narrow it and confuse it through cold examination: *Who is my neighbor?* To show him that this only apparent confusion requires absolutely no complicated scrutiny, but is simply understood by the heart, Christ tells a parable of the mercy of a wanderer to a man who was beaten and stripped by robbers on the road.

Luke 10:29

He sees priests and Levites who are not ready enough, not assiduous enough, to help the poor man. To incline them to mercy at least through shame, he shows them in the parable that the priest and Levite walked by the afflicted man, but a Samaritan, who was the most despised kind of person by the Jews, helped the helpless man as though he were his servant or relative.

Neither does the divine Teacher of mercy leave *the tax collectors and the sinners [who] drew near to Him to hear Him* without a word of instruction. These, both in unlawful gains and in ill usage of their ill-gotten money, were directed only by earthly wisdom, which supposes that giving money to others is useful only insofar as it can be used for greater gains later, or to protect oneself from future need. Christ teaches them also with a parable, and he tells them of an unrighteous steward, adding at the end this instruction: *And I say to you, make friends for yourselves by unrighteous mammon, that when you fail, they may receive you into an everlasting home.*

Luke 15:1

Luke 16:9

Evidently, those who listened to this instruction understood it not with their earthly mindset—the divine Teacher never taught to that kind of mindset—but with the reasoning of a pure, spir-

itual wisdom, because the Knower of hearts did not find it necessary to add anything to protect this teaching from an incorrect interpretation. Is that because some Christians will not easily enter into the true mindset of Christ's teaching, as these tax-collectors did? I would prefer to say that this would be impossible, but sometimes I hear questions such as these: what does the parable of the unjust steward mean? What does it mean to make friends by unrighteous mammon? Is it possible that he who acquired his riches unjustly, having given alms from his ill-gotten money, can thereby prepare for himself a mansion for eternity?

I think it necessary to resolve this confusion. For this reason, we must have a clearer understanding of the context of the parable.

A certain man had a steward who took care of his large agricultural holdings. When the master found out that this steward was wasting the money entrusted to him, he decided to dismiss him from his duties. For this reason, he demanded a full account of the steward's work. The steward, seeing that he was about to lose both his place and his money, called all the people to whom he loaned bread and oil. Then he told them to rewrite the account of the debts to make it seem like they owed less than they actually did. By doing this, he effectively gifted one person five hundred measures of oil, and another twenty measures of wheat. He hoped that when he lost his place and money, the grateful debtors would accept him into their households.

So the master commended the unjust steward because he had dealt shrewdly. Notice that the unjust steward was not commended for lying, which is never commendable (and for which he was already condemned to be dismissed), but for "dealing shrewdly."

Luke 16:8

To correctly understand this parable, we must take into account a general rule about the genre of parables. The image offered by the parable, in essence, cannot be completely identical with the object that it symbolizes. In the same way, not everything in the telling of the story need apply to the final meaning and interpretation. For example, in the parable of the unjust judge *who did not fear God nor regard man,* the judge finally listens to the widow who constantly, every day, begged for his protection. In the final analysis of the parable, two aspects are of importance: first, the fact that the man was a judge; second, that God always hears and fulfills a prayer that is offered insistently and constantly. However, the details of the first part of the parable (that is, the fact that the judge is an unjust man who does not fear God nor regard men) have nothing to do with the meaning of the parable. After all, these are human qualities that evidently have nothing to do with the holiness of God the Judge.

Luke 18:2

Similarly, the incorrect or unlawful aspects of the parable of the unjust steward are only details necessary to give credence to a story from everyday life. As for the message of the parable, these details are superfluous, since they are not compatible with the spirit of Christ's teaching.

The true meaning of the parable is determined by the following details. The steward manages another man's estate. Similarly, every person in this world uses the riches and other gifts of God's creation and providence, not as an independent master, accountable to no one, but as a steward who will have to give an account to God, for to Him alone does everything belong originally and essentially. Finally, the steward must leave behind his position of authority and give an account. Similarly, every human being, at the end of his earthly life, must leave behind everything that he had on earth and stand before the judgment of God to give an account. The dismissed steward saw that he would be left without money or home. Similarly, those who leave earthly life—some in good time, coming to know themselves in humility; others, too late—realize that they are lacking in asceticism and virtues, that they did not acquire enough faith and love for God, that they did not strengthen themselves enough in prayer, and that they did not perform enough labors of moderation and self-rejection; nor did they suffer for the truth, which would have thrown open the doors to one of the mansions in heaven.

What is the poor steward to do? What is the poor soul to do? The steward has hopes to be accepted into the homes of those whom he favored by sharing from the abundance entrusted to him. The soul, though it did not reach perfection, hopes that the poor and sorrowful to whom it gave help and consolation from its earthly prosperity will help open the gates of eternal rest—which the poor acquire through their endurance in patience—through their grace-filled prayers of faith.

The final words of the parable clearly show that it uses human wisdom to symbolize spiritual wisdom, but in no way mixes them up: *The sons of this world are more shrewd in their generation than the sons of light.* In other words, Christ regrets that the sons of worldly wisdom are talented enough, even in the midst of their fall, to use ill means to ensure their temporary survival, while the sons of light, the disciples of divine wisdom, often are not diligent enough, even in the light and with its power, to lay down the correct path to the eternal mansions! *Luke 16:8*

All that is left is to explain the expression "unrighteous mammon," lest a word badly understood dim the purity of the divine teaching.

The Syrians had an idol called "Mammon," and it was superstitiously considered the god of riches. The god of riches was thus later equated with the riches themselves: mammon is "money." The Lord, of course, not without reason, instead of using the word "riches," used the name "mammon," in which the idea of riches is combined with the idea of idol-worship. The reason is clear: Christ speaks here not only about riches, but about riches that are gathered with a passionate attachment, making them unrighteous or even impure. For in the language of Scripture, "unrighteousness" can indicate vice in general, just as "righteousness" indicates virtue in general.

Thus, what does the expression *make friends for yourselves by unrighteous mammon* mean? It means: riches quickly become unrighteous mammon because of your passionate attachment to them. They become objects of vice, idols. You should transform such riches into positive gain by giving them to the poor, thereby winning in them spiritual friends and petitioners before God for the sake of your salvation.

As for those rich men who not only are not free from unrighteous, passionate attachment to riches, but are also burdened by the fact that their riches are ill-gotten, in vain do they seek an easy path to covering their sin in the parable of the unjust steward. However, if they truly want an instruction that applies to them specifically, they will find it in the story of Zaccheus the publican. He extirpates two sins in his conversion. First of all, he washes away his passionate attachment to money by almsgiving: *Look, Lord, I give half of my goods to the poor.* But his heavier sin of ill-gotten gains he washes away by a fair compensation to those whom he robbed: *If I have taken anything from anyone by false accusation, I restore fourfold.*

The wise Jesus ben Sirach ascribes to mercy the dignity of sacrifice and divine service: *He who does alms sacrifices a praise offering.* However, this offering before God must be pure, not only of iniquity, but of baseness as well: *You shall not bring the wages of a harlot or the price of a dog to the house of the Lord your God for any vowed offering, for both of these are an abomination to the Lord your God.* This is how you must determine that the money you give in alms be sourced from a pure spring.

At the same time, it comes to mind to ask this question. Do people do well when they gather money, saying that they are collecting money for some play or other useless frivolity, but promise that half of the gathered money will be used for charity? What will happen then? Will the almsgiving wash away the vanity? Or will the vanity cancel out the alms? Can we find an answer that is more pleasant to the ear than the question? However, there can be no doubt that if the money allotted for charitable entertainment were redirected completely to almsgiving, and the entertainment were canceled to boot, then the almsgiving would be twice as great and incomparably more pure. The Apostle teaches us to *weep with those who weep*, not to rejoice at the thought of the miserable, nor to overfill the cup of enjoyment just so that the spillover would be left to the sorrowful. *Romans 12:15*

Then again, I hope that no one will be offended by my concern that the resourceful talents of the charitable, though well intentioned, could have much greater dignity in the ways and means that they act.

Let us calm the storm of our thoughts and words, subjecting both to the unquestionable general rule: *Honor the Lord with your possessions, and with the first-fruits of all your increase,* both in terms of your works of piety and your works of mercy toward your neighbor. Amen. *Proverbs 3:9*

11

On the Faith of those Who Seek to Touch Jesus (1825)

"And the whole multitude sought to touch Him, for power went out from Him and healed them all." (Luke 6:19)

What a miraculous spectacle we see in the account of the holy Evangelist Luke! The Lord Jesus, after praying all night, and after choosing His twelve Apostles in the morning, came down to a level place. The Apostles followed Him, and the assembly of all His other disciples met and greeted Him. A great multitude of people surrounded Him, not only from Jerusalem but from all Judea, and even from the sea-coast cities of Tyre and Sidon. They wanted to hear His teaching. They wanted to be healed of their diseases.

What did the crowd do? It jostled to get nearer to the Teacher and Healer, no longer just to hear or ask, not to beg for healing and the laying on of hands or a word that would forgive their sins. No, they all threw themselves toward Him as they could, just to touch either His life-giving body or His sanctified clothes, or, so to speak, power-imbued clothes: *for power went out from Him and healed them all.* *Luke 6:19*

It is a truly miraculous spectacle, worthy not merely of wonder, but pious contemplation, and not merely contemplation, but emulation. Who would not desire to touch the Savior, from whom power goes out, power that heals all? Let us read the Gospel to see how this can be achieved, and we will know that we must also touch Christ with faith.

In order for those who desired to come into contact with Jesus Christ to achieve their desire, His mercy is required, and it is an extreme mercy. When He was on the mountain, they could not touch Him, for they probably did not even know where to find Him. He had to first come down from the mountain to a level place where the people awaited Him. This descent was only a small, physical symbol of the greater, multi-faceted mercy of Christ's descent to man's level. Consider what He had to leave behind on the mountain—a blessed and pleasant, prayerful conversation with His heavenly Father. And yet, He descended.

And what will He find below? A mix of people, among whom some listen to Him, while others, perhaps, are trying to catch Him in some false teaching. Every person is eager to approach Him with his own needs; however, there are probably some who do not know what it is they ask. In the multitude of those who seek to touch Him, there are likely some sick people whom we would not like to approach (though we are stricken with similar ailments). There are also sinners from whom we (though we are equally sinners) would turn away, if we could see their hearts as He does. And yet, He descends. He approaches.

And what else? These unfortunate, perishing souls who have need of Him as their Helper and Savior seem to approach Him without the reverence required before such a divine Miracle-worker. Evidently, they act without consideration of any normal rules of civility and respect. They "thronged" and "pressed Him," as St. Luke expressed it in a different episode. Those who *Luke 8:45* are disfigured by diseases and covered with open sores throw themselves at Him indiscriminately. The possessed are dragged and pressed into Him by others. And yet, He endures it all. He has mercy on all. As a pure and deep river accepts all who drink from it without becoming upset or lessened, so the infinite salvific power of the Lord allows all to approach Him, and His power is not lessened for their multitude or their unworthiness. *For power went out from Him and healed them all.*

Luke 6:19

Christians! If we need the mercy of our divine Savior, so that we may be able to touch Him to our salvation—and without a doubt we do need it!—then He will never deny us. Not only did he descend from the mountain to a level place that could hold several thousand people from Judea and the neighboring countries, but He also descended from the heights of heaven for all the millions of people who lived, live, and who will ever live on this earth. Since His divine power, being more exalted and pure than the heavens, was completely unattainable for fallen and unworthy human nature, He lowered this power into human nature itself. He poured it into a vessel of flesh similar to our own in all, except sin. To heal our body of sin, we especially need that power. In the excess of His mercy to us, He, so to speak, overfilled the vessel of His most-pure body with His divine power, so that it poured over through His very clothes and healed the woman with an issue of blood.

When, after His Resurrection from the dead, all authority was given Him *in heaven and on earth,* when He raised up our assumed flesh with Himself and seated it at the right hand of God the Father, then *He who descended* and *ascended far above all the heavens... fill[ed] all things.* Consequently, He filled the entire earth and all times with His divine, salvific, physically, and especially spiritually, "all-healing power."

Matthew 28:18

Ephesians 4:10

Do you desire, even now, a physical proof of the intimacy and mercy of Jesus Christ toward us? We have such proof every day on this very altar, where He always, as before, with His divine and salvific power, through the *fullness of the Godhead* that dwells in Him *bodily*, allows us not only to touch Him, but to eat His body and drink His blood, in the appearance of bread and wine, for healing and life eternal.

Colossians 2:9

We also see in the Gospel that for us to touch Him unto our salvation, He needed to condescend to our level. But we must also seek Him and approach Him. *The whole multitude sought to touch Him.* This seeking and this approaching must not be understood only physically. There were those who sought Jesus—to kill Him. There were those who approached Him—to strike Him on the cheek. Without a doubt, His all-healing power did not pour itself out for the sake of these people. Christ Himself clearly distinguished the humble approach to be healed from all other kinds of approaches. After all, in the midst of a crowd of people jostling Him, he felt no one approach His healing power except for a single woman. *But Jesus said, 'Somebody touched Me, for I perceived power going out from Me.'*

Luke 6:19

Luke 8:46

What defines this special kind of approach to Christ, accompanied not by dead brazenness, but living contact that elicited the outpouring of salvific power from Him? The Lord also clearly shows us the answer through the example of the woman with the issue of blood, who, from among the many who approached and touched Him, alone received healing. For what did He say to her? *Daughter, be of good cheer; your faith has made you well.* Thus, that which appeared to the physical eyes to be a mere approach and a touch, the Lord calls, according to spiritual understanding, *faith.* This is why the Lord poured out His power over the great multitude and healed every single one of them. They sought Him with faith, they approached Him with faith, and with faith did they spiritually come into contact with His power as they bodily touched His all-pure body and robes.

Luke 8:48

Luke 6

Thus, *the whole multitude sought to touch Him*, or at least those from the crowd who were models of faith for the rest. And what

Luke 6:19

faith is evident in these people! Not that weak and barely visible faith that needed to be sought out by the Lord Himself in the two blind men when He asked them, *Do you believe that I am able to do this?* Not that weak and vacillating faith of the man with the possessed boy who asked the Lord for help that he did not hope to receive: *If You can do anything, have compassion on us and help us.* This man claimed to have faith, and yet did not believe his own assertion: *Lord, I believe; help my unbelief!* Not that slow and half-dead faith of the blind man in Bethsaida who, after the Lord even spit in his eyes and twice laid His hands on him, barely awoke to the realization of his own healing.

Matthew 9:28

Mark 9:22
Mark 9:24

The faith of those who seek to touch Jesus does not wait to be aroused by Him. It does not waver in doubt of His power. It is not disturbed by thoughts of its own unworthiness. It does not require of Him any action other than a word. It firmly, freely goes straight to the Source of grace and drinks from it. It is as though it takes the all-healing power of the Savior by force. *For power went out from Him and healed them all.* What was it that unleashed the torrent of this healing power? Nothing other than the extreme boldness of the people's faith: *the whole multitude sought to touch Him.*

Luke 6:19

Luke 6:19

After this, O Christian, if you say that you would desire to be found worthy of the salvific touch of the Lord, then my answer to you is not difficult. Seek, approach, and touch; only seek with faith, approach with faith, and touch Him with faith. Do you ask where you can find the Lord? How you can approach and touch Him? Seek Him with your thoughts in heaven, with love in your heart, and with reverence in the Church. Seek Him everywhere with the deeds that you attempt and accomplish in His name. Approach Him as did the multitude who believed in Him, with a desire to hear Him. This desire healed them, that is, through instruction by His word and through prayer to Him. Touch Him in the holy Mysteries, through which He invests His divine and salvific power to the Church. And most importantly, touch Him in the sacrament of His body and blood.

Whether or not you succeed in your search depends on you. It is up to your will to determine whether you will benefit much or a little from approaching and touching the Lord, for your salvation and blessedness. No matter what your spiritual ailments, the more complete your faith, the more completely will you be healed of them by the power of Christ, which will illumine the blind eye of your mind with the knowledge of the truth, and which will mobilize the paralyzed strength of your spirit for virtue, and which will deliver you from the tempting spirits, and which will resurrect you from dead deeds to a spiritual and holy life. However, if you seek without attentiveness, if you approach Him only with your lips, if you touch His holiness only superficially, without living faith and zeal, then you will be like that crowd that only pressed Jesus as He went but did not acquire His salvific power.

The Lord Himself gives a stern rebuke to those who seek Him incorrectly, that is, without faith: *Most assuredly, I say to you, you seek Me, not because you saw the signs, but because you ate of the loaves and were filled.* John 6:26

Oh, I would wish that none of you who have come today to seek the Lord in this church deserve a similar rebuke because of your inattentiveness to the treasure house of faith and grace, through seeking only visible and temporary goods and sensual consolations! Let us remember also this instruction of the Lord, together with His rebuke: *Do not labor for the food which perishes,* do the *works of God,* for *this is the work of God, that you believe in Him whom He sent.* John 6:27-29

Amen.

12

On Cheesefare Sunday Against Intemperance (1827)

"But take heed to yourselves, lest your hearts be weighed down with carousing, drunkenness, and cares of this life, and that Day come on you unexpectedly." (Luke 21:34)

The approaching time of Lent calls us to temperance. The holy Church has arranged these preparatory days by degrees, so that, little by little removing the heaviness of food and increasing our labors of prayer, it may raise us to the perfection of Lent and to its prolonged ascetical labors of repentance and prayer. However, at this threshold of holy Lent through which we are passing this moment, thoughtless custom has introduced so much that is contrary to temperance and sobriety, both of mind and spirit! It seems to me that these customs must inspire within us both remorse and zeal, like the zeal for the house of God that inspired the Lord to make a whip and drive out of the threshold of the Temple all those who bought and sold, transforming the house of prayer into a house of merchandise and a haven for thieves. O, if only

He would help us with a small whip woven together from words of truth and chastity, if not to cast out completely, then at least to lessen the intemperance that especially rages at the doorway to the holy sanctum of Lent! Moreover, this intemperance often oppresses the body, empties the soul, depletes our stores of grace, scatters abroad our virtues, and buries our talents!

Take heed to yourselves, says the Lord, *lest your heart be weighed down with carousing and drunkenness.* Will not this warning seem excessive to some? Will not some be offended even at the suspicion of such crude vices? I do not desire to suspect or offend anyone. However, I remind all of you, people who consider yourselves to be properly temperate and sober, that the Lord gave this warning originally to His chosen disciples. This instruction, which was not offensive to Peter, James, John, or Andrew, cannot be offensive or excessive to any of us. *Luke 21:34*

What is gluttony? Is it a state when our body can no longer fit in any food? What is drunkenness? Is it a state when our mind is drowning in wine, and our body can no longer hold up our heavy head? If—and it is not difficult to be certain of this—the real purpose of food and drink is the sustenance and renewal of the body (which unnoticeably yet constantly swallows up perishable things); and if the taste of food and the pleasantness of drink are given only as a means to this end, then every bit of food that exceeds the simple satisfaction of hunger, to be savored for its flavor—this is gluttony. Every sip of a drink that exceeds the simple quenching of thirst, to be drunk for pleasure—this is drunkenness.

What about our tables, which are so full of different dishes that we can hardly count them, can hardly guess at their composition, and can hardly even name them? Are these not subtle snares that we set for each other, to catch our neighbor in gluttony, no matter how subtle, and in drunkenness, no matter how apparently sober? You will not even notice that you have passed from eating to gluttony, how a simple drink has become drunkenness. We must be diligently attentive to ourselves. *Take heed to yourselves.*

How many different arts, objects, and tools does the reasoning man use, only to fill his small and inanimate stomach! How humiliating it is for the intellect, when it is wasted in various contrivances, only to pay a daily tribute demanded by the stomach! It is like an implacable master that wants everything as refined as possible, in as large an amount as possible! And how the stomach mocks the enslaved reason of man when the final result of all man's efforts and refined cooking end up in impurity and filth!

Stand up, you pitiful worshipper of the stomach! If you cannot raise your eyes higher than yourself, then at least stand in front of the mirror and look at yourself. Is not the law against slavery to the stomach obvious in your own body? Don't you see that your chest is higher than your stomach? In the chest resides the heart that desires good and that feels love. And above the chest is the head, crowned by the mind that contemplates truth, and the intellect that imagines all possibilities. Can you not see that your dark stomach, which can neither think nor desire, is under both the head and the chest, as hell is under both heaven and earth? Do you need a great deal of perspicacity to notice that it must not lord it over the higher regions, but rather be in service and subjugation to them? If, on the contrary, you try to constantly please the stomach, giving it what it blindly demands; if you desire for it and think on its behalf, then beware, lest it become stronger and higher than your own head. For then, with its repugnant heaviness, it will oppress and constrain the noble actions of the mind and heart. *Take heed to yourselves,* says the Lord, *lest your heart be weighed down with carousing and drunkenness.*

By *heart,* the Lord means in general the "inner reality" of man, which we can see from His own words in a different place. In this passage, He combines these terms, using them to describe each other: *For from within, out of the heart of man, proceed evil thoughts...* Thus, both *heart* and the inner part of man indicate the spiritual powers of man, with their actions and perfections, especially the reasoning will, the power to desire, and the capability of understanding. This is what the overwhelming heaviness of an overfilled stomach can finally destroy in you. *Take heed to yourselves, lest your heart be weighed down.*

Mark 7:21

Luke 21:34

Perhaps some will say that they do not notice that people who are less temperate than others are then less capable of using their reason and the power of their will. I do not argue that some of them are even more capable of using their mind to understand and invent ever more refined pleasures for the senses and the imagination. These are dragged toward their desires more powerfully than others. The spirit of such people hovers like steam over warmed-up food, or maybe slightly higher. However, when it's necessary to raise one's thoughts and hearts on high, higher than the visible heavens—which though are subtle, are still physical, and so lower than the domain proper to the purified spirit—when it's necessary to direct one's desire toward God, then it turns out that the stomach, weighed down by overeating, hangs like a barbell under the wings of the spirit, pulling it down to the earth. Thus, no matter what the effort, such a person falls to the ground more than he flies to the heavens. Fat animals that eat large quantities of food cannot run as fast as the deer, which eats little. In the same way, a glutton cannot be as active or prosperous in ascetic labors as a temperate man.

You know that man fell. But how? Was it not his stomach, weighed down by eating the forbidden fruit, that cast him down out of the blessed paradise to the miserable earth? If you weigh it down even more, it will pull you down from the earth into the depths of hell. Truly, what was it that led to Sodom's horrifying destruction? *Look*, says the prophet, *this was the iniquity of your sister Sodom: She and her daughter had pride, fullness of food, and abundance of idleness.*

The Lord warns that a similar, but even more horrible, calamity will befall the gluttons: *That Day [will] come on you unexpectedly.* What day? A day which was only prefigured in a diminutive simile by the judgment on Sodom. This day is not a doom on a single or several luxurious and sensual cities, but the entire cosmos. It will force *men's hearts [to fail] from fear and the expectation of those things which are coming on the earth,* for on this day *the Lord comes with ten thousand of His saints, to execute judgment on all, to convict all who are ungodly among them of all their ungodly deeds which they have committed in an ungodly way, and of all the harsh things which ungodly sinners have spoken against Him.*

The Lord constantly exhorts us that this terrible day will be especially unexpected to those who are dedicated to intemperance, luxury, and caring for the advantages and pleasure of this life. *For as in the days before the flood, they were eating and drinking, marrying and giving in marriage, until the day that Noah entered the ark, and did not know until the flood came and took them all away, so also will the coming of the Son of Man be. Likewise as it was also in the days of Lot: They ate, they drank, they bought, they sold, they planted, they built; but on the day that Lot went out of Sodom it rained fire and brimstone from heaven and destroyed them all. Even so will it be in the day when the Son of Man is revealed.*

Truly, the people whose mouths open not to praise the glory of God or utter before God the desires of their hearts, but only to swallow and turn into corruption, like a tomb, all that is best among the living and growing things on this earth; the people who spend half their life in the labor of burdening their stomach, and the other dragging that burden around; the people who let wine enflame their blood and confuse their head—what time do they have to think of heavenly matters, to penetrate the hidden depths of the judgments of God, to deeply contemplate the

SERMON 12: ON CHEESEFARE SUNDAY. AGAINST INTEMPERANCE

words of the prophets, to pay attention to the signs of the times, to stand guard in expectation of the imminent kingdom of God, which is completely foreign to them, since it is *not eating and drinking*? *Romans 14:17*

But here is something even more terrifying. This predominating sensuality, this forgetfulness of God and lack of temperance are not merely subject to the judgment and justice of God at the most unexpected moment. They are also, according to the word of the Lord, a kind of foreshadowing or a threshold of the final judgment: if *your hearts be weighed down with…drunkenness…the day [will] come on you unexpectedly*. What should we think, then, when we see that the rich man and the poor, whether in a home or in a tavern, whether early or late, constantly labor for their stomach? What should we think when the stomach swallows up all great gains and inheritances, when people who labor hard for daily bread waste the limited fruits of their labor and sweat on excess and intemperance—whether crude or refined, it doesn't matter—or on caprices that are not required or even known in nature? What do we do when the announcement of the feast and the foreshadowing of the coming fast—which are, in the Church's intention, tools for the exaltation of reverence and piety—are transformed into tools for gluttony, like the holy vessels that were used to decorate the feast of Belshazzar? How dangerous this is, for *the day [will] come on you unexpectedly*. *Luke 21:34*

Luke 21:34

Let us take care, brothers, that we eat and drink to the glory of God, not to our detriment or to offend the Provider of good things, who is God. Satisfy your hunger and thirst but do not raise arms against temperance and fasting. Let man's daily bread strengthen his heart; let wine in moderation give joy to the heart of the sorrowful or give strength to the weak. *Go your way, eat,* let us say, if necessary, together with Nehemiah and Ezra, *eat the fat, drink the sweet,* but only as a sign that *this day is holy to our Lord.* Let it not be untimely or without moderation, like those *whose god is their belly.* At all times, listen to the words of the Lord and *Nehemiah 8:10*

Philippians 3:19

take heed to yourselves, lest your hearts be weighed down with carousing, drunkenness, and cares of this life, and that day [of judgment] come on you unexpectedly. Instead, let our hearts be like the oil lamps of the wise virgins, full of the oil of grace, burning with love, and alight with faith. Let us be ready to meet the Judge like a Bridegroom, and to feast with Him in the heavenly bridal chamber for all ages! Amen.

Luke 21:34

13

On the Proper Preparation for Prayer (1844)

"Before you pray, prepare yourself; and do not become like a man who tempts the Lord." (Sirach 18:23)[4]

How pleasant is the view of a field of wheat. Rustled by a gentle wind, an entire field bows low. Equally pleasant is the view of a church filled with people praying. The Spirit of God blows through them, producing meek movements of the heart and offers their good fruits to God and His sacraments. I do not merely invent this image, for it is found in the Gospel. The teaching of the Gospel is likened to a seed, the preacher of the Gospel is likened to a sower, the listeners of the Gospel are likened to soil being prepared for sowing, and those who have come to believe are likened to a planted field that *yields crops by itself: first the blade, then the head, after that the full grain in the head.*

Mark 4:28

---

4   This translation corresponds to the Masoretic text, not the LXX. However, the LXX version has a different meaning, so we include the Masoretic, as intended by Metropolitan Philaret.

However, I must admit that this same parable that, like a mirror, doubles the pleasure of what I see before me here in church, also does not allow me to carelessly remain in pleasant contemplation. *The earth yields crops by itself: first the blade, then the head, after that the full grain in the head.* Thus, the young blade without a head makes me think of those souls who are yet young in Christianity and so do not yet bear fruit of the Spirit. But there are also, sometimes, heads without grain. These are the souls who have the external appearance of piety without its inner content. A head of wheat without grain looks like a full head; likewise, the image of piety looks like true piety—how delusive this is! The longer a head of wheat does not fill with grain, the closer it comes to a fate of final "grainlessness" or uselessness for the granary. The longer a person remains in a purely superficial state of piety, without filling up its inner meaning, the closer he comes to a final ossification in this spiritual state of fruitlessness, in which nothing useful for the kingdom of heaven will be found in him. How dangerous this is! And at the same time, this is what most inspires worry in me: the wheat is not at fault if the sky and the earth do not fill it with grain. However, heaven is always ready with its grace-filled influence to fill a person with good fruits. It is the fault of the person himself if he is slothful in attracting this influence through faith, prayer, and a total dedication to the influence of heaven.

Mark 4:28

"But what can I do? I pray, and I call down the influence of heaven. And yet, it is not in my power to make my prayer effective." Is this not what some people, or perhaps most people, think? In answer to this, I offer you the instruction of the Wise Man (Jesus ben Sirach) concerning that which is in our power to make our prayer God-pleasing: *Before you pray, prepare yourself; and do not become like a man who tempts the Lord.*

Sirach 18:23

There is no point in being astounded if you cannot accomplish the work you attempt if you do it willy-nilly, haphazardly. If you want to win in battle, you have to prepare the right armor and train in the proper use of arms. If you want to swim across a river, you have to first prepare yourself by taking off your clothes, which would weigh you down and cause you to sink. Similarly, if you want to pray beneficially and successfully, "before you pray, prepare yourself."

What is the proper preparation for prayer?

Shall we say the following? 1) We must believe that God's providence is accomplished in us, not only through the laws of nature but independent of those laws, by the all-powerful will of God. 2) The will of God, thanks to His love for man, comes down to our own will to help it be accomplished. 3) God not only allows, but desires us to raise our impure desires up to Him in prayer. 4) We must trust that despite our worthlessness by nature, despite our unworthiness due to sin, God, by His limitless mercy, does not reject our prayer, as the word of the Lord witnesses, *If you then, being evil, know how to give good gifts to your children, how much more will your Father who is in heaven give good things...the Holy Spirit to those who ask Him!* 5) We must, according to the words and example of David, *foresee the Lord always before me*, knowing with firm conviction that God, invisibly but actively, presides over my prayer, sees me, hears me, and tests my heart to reward me according to what is in my heart.

Matthew 7:11, Luke 11:13, Psalm 15:

But all this should be already well-known to every person who prays. These are such preparatory dispositions to prayer without which prayer will not only be ineffectual, but will hardly be prayer at all.

There are other preparations for prayer whose necessity perhaps we have not considered or have forgotten, without which prayer can begin and perhaps continue for a time, but such prayer will not have true and complete success.

One of these preparations for prayer is forgiveness of enemies and making peace with all our neighbors, that is, with all mankind. For what do you say in that prayer that should be strange to no one, in which nothing can be changed, for it is the model prayer given by the Lord Himself, complete in itself and appropriate for every human being? You say, *Forgive us our trespasses as we forgive those who trespass against us.* If you say this without especial attention, without preliminary testing of your own heart, then it can easily happen that during your prayer, you may be hiding enmity or offenses against your neighbor. Consequently, when you ask God to forgive you as you forgive others, you are actually asking God to *not* forgive you as you do *not* forgive your neighbor. To avoid this sin, which evidently opposes the action of prayer, we must carefully test the disposition of our heart. And a merely mental examination of our heart is not trustworthy. We can only be sure that we have made peace with everything if in actual deed we have done everything in our power to make such reconciliation and peace possible. This carefulness, this preparation for prayer, is so necessary that the Lord commands us to stop praying if we don't have peace in our heart: *Therefore if you bring your gift to the altar, and there remember that your brother has something against you, leave your gift there before the altar, and go your way. First be reconciled to your brother, and then come and offer your gift.*

Matthew 6:12

Matthew 5:23-24

Let us pay attention to how strict is the law concerning reconciliation. *If you...remember that your brother has something against you*—this can be true even when you find nothing to fault yourself with regarding your brother. But the Lord does not allay the requirement to seek reconciliation, even in such a case. *First be reconciled to your brother.* What is the purpose of such strictness, some may ask. Why can I not pray without worrying about what others think about me? To these questions, I can simply answer, "I do not know." The commandment of the Lord does not lose its power because of my ignorance. If a creditor of a debt for which you can lawfully languish in prison to the end of your days offered you forgiveness of the debt, but under the condition that you forgive an insignificant debt to your neighbor, you would be mad not to accept such an easy and beneficial condition only

Matthew 5:23

Matthew 5:24

because you don't understand the reason for it. Similarly, when God forgives sins—for which we should be punished with eternal death—under the condition that you forgive your neighbor some small insult, to reconcile with him after some kind of misunderstanding, you would be mad to deprive yourself of the great forgiveness of God only because you cannot understand why He so insistently requires this small forgiveness of your neighbor's sin, this simple reconciliation.

What is the need, you ask, for this strictness with which the labor of reconciliation is required of you? A not insignificant need, for the intentions of God are never insignificant. This strictness is a mercy, and a greater one than you imagine. You want to be successful, and you want to pray for success? God wants more than that. He wants all His creation to prosper, as much as they are able to. Therefore, He wants you to succeed, but your brother as well, even one who "has something against you," for he could be distressed by this, or, which is the same thing, not spiritually prospering. If you seek reconciliation with your miserable brother with love and humility, then you will free his heart from the splinter of enmity or sorrow. It will become more still and purer than before. In this way, you will be a servant of the providence of God in the work of the spiritual progress of your brother. Do you see how important and wonderful is this need that requires of you the labor of reconciliation? Do you understand how in the strictness of requirement is found the mercy of God?

Do you say, "Why can I not pray without worrying about what others think of me?" Because, if you do not care for the brother who "has something against you," then you do not care for the stillness of his spirit, the purity of his heart, and, consequently, his prosperity. And if you do not care for his prosperity, then you do not love him. But, according to the witness of the Apostle John, *He who does not love his brother abides in death.* A dead man can do nothing; consequently, you, being spiritually dead as one who does not love, cannot accomplish the spiritual work of

1 John 3:14

prayer as you ought to. For whatever keeps your heart closed to your neighbor is not love, and it keeps it closed to God as well. Go and reconcile with your brother. Place in your heart the spark of pure love. This spark will help your prayer arise as incense before God.

Another preparation important for success in prayer is a sincere desire and firm intention to leave behind any sin to which we are attached, and to live by the will of God alone.

Return to the Most High and turn away from wrongdoing, and hate an abomination exceedingly. And the Apostle Paul puts at the foundation of any spiritual building of God within man the following seal: *Let everyone who names the name of Christ depart from iniquity.* It is as if he said, "If you call on the name of the Lord in confession, in exhortation, in prayer, and you depart from iniquity, then in you is a firm foundation and a true sign of the new person who is being saved, whom God will recreate through His grace from an old and perishing man. If you will not depart with a firm will from iniquity, then even if you call on the name of the Lord, your foundation is not strong, your sign is dubious, and your prayer does not so much lack power as it lacks purity. As Solomon said, *He who turns away his ear so as not to hear the law, He also makes his prayer repulsive.*

Therefore, it is no surprise if the Lord does not hear such prayers with any intention of granting the petition. On the contrary, He turns away from such prayers. *But why do you call Me 'Lord, Lord' and not do the things which I say?* When the Prophet Isaiah heard the complaints of the Jews concerning their lack of success in prayer, he exhorted them thus concerning this futility: *Behold, the Lord's hand is not shortened, that it cannot save; nor His ear heavy, that it cannot hear. But your iniquities have separated you from your God; and your sins have hidden His face from you, so that He will not hear. For your hands are defiled with blood, and your fingers with iniquity; your lips have spoken lies, your tongue has muttered perversity.*

Sirach 17:21

2 Timothy 2:19

Proverbs 28:9

Luke 6:46

Isaiah 59:1-3

What hope can I have, says the sinner, if my very prayer, by which I hope to ask forgiveness of sins, is not accepted by God? I answer thus. Your hope is that very prayer, but combined with unchangeable repentance and resolute abandonment of sin.

But how can I free myself from sin without the grace of God, which I desire to acquire through prayer? Truly, you cannot free yourself from sin without the grace of God. However, the grace of God cannot free you from sin without your will, because grace does not want to force itself on your will. It does not want to take away from you the wonderful gift of freedom, which you have used so badly, having sold yourself willingly to slavery to sin for the sake of evanescent and delusive pleasures. Do what little you can, and then pray. Grace will accomplish its greatness in you. Leave sin behind and resolve never to sin again, and then pray. Grace will then actively free you from the lordship of sin. Abandon your willful sin, and then pray. Grace will then also preserve you from involuntary sin, and you will not bear the guilt of the involuntarily performed sin. Purge sin from your heart. Do not love it, but come to hate it. Cut sin out of your mind. Try not to think of its pleasure, and then pray. Grace will then help you acquire a pure heart, a pure mind, a pure soul and body, and a pure life.

Whoever has not prepared himself preliminarily with such dispositions and approaches prayer; whoever asks for mercies and benefits from God without thinking about how not to offend Him with repeated sins—he truly, as the wise man explained, is "like a man who tempts the Lord." For if you were to utter not merely the words of prayer, but everything that hides in your heart without a desire for correction, then what would that sound like? "Lord, forgive me the sins by which I offended Thee, though I have no intention of stopping similar offenses. Fulfill my desire, though I do not promise to do Thy will." If you were to utter similar speeches to an earthly lord or a judge, would not any person in his right mind accept this not as a petition, but as a foolish attempt to irritate and anger? How much more of this kind of tempter is one who stands before God with words of prayer on his mouth but a rebellious spirit in his heart, a brazen man who tempts the Lord to the limit of His longsuffering endurance? This endurance lasts a very long time, if such a petitioner is not struck down by the justice of God. And of course, this state is nowhere near the kind of prayer that is filled with grace and fulfilled by God.

O Christian! Do not be like the man who tempts the Lord. Do not bring your anger before the face of the all-good One. Do not bring impurity before the face of the all-pure One. *Before you pray, prepare yourself.* Fill your oil lamp with oil, so that it will burn brightly and for a long time. Fill your heart with peace, so that your prayer will be bright and constant. Hurry to diligently remove all the foulness of an impure and uncorrected life from your spiritual censer. Be faithful and diligent in these early preparations for your prayer, and the Spirit of God, who is the Spirit of prayer, through intercessions for you in groanings that cannot be uttered, will teach you how to perfect this spiritual labor. Then you may bear divine fruit, which will be harvested in eternal life. Amen.

Sirach 18:23

14

On the Lord's Prayer

*But why do you call Me "Lord, Lord,"
and not do the things which I say? (Luke 6:46)*

The Lord's terrifying wrath reveals itself before us, dear listeners, in this utterance from the Gospel! It rebukes not only those who blaspheme or forget His holy Name, but even those who would seem to bear the name of God on their lips with piety! *Why do you call me "Lord, Lord?"*   Luke 6:46

So, is it possible to insult God with prayer? Yes. It is possible if the prayer of our lips is not accompanied by the prayer of the heart, and if the prayer of our heart is not followed by the prayer of action. *Why do you call me "Lord, Lord," and not do the thing which I say?*   Luke 6:46

When the Prophet David described the rejection of Judas the traitor, he cried out in ecstatic anger: *Let his prayer be turned into sin!* But the prayer of Judas—if he even prayed—should have been the most holy prayer, for he, like we also, learned from the Son of God Himself how to call upon *Our Father, who art in heaven.* Thus, should not others worry about saying this most holy and divine prayer of the Lord in an unworthy and improper manner?   Psalm 108:7

Matthew 6:9

Let us consider the proper and salvific way of praying the Lord's prayer.

Our Father, who art in heaven! we utter, emulating the Only-begotten One.

And yes, I do say "emulating the Only-begotten One." For who would dare utter such an invocation if the Only-begotten One did not become *the firstborn among many brethren* and did not put on our own flesh? Who would dare use such words if we all did not put Him on through baptism? The daughters of Eve give birth only to slaves and sons of wrath. The Church alone gives birth to children of freedom and grace. Our birth into slavery is unwilling; our birth into freedom must be free. Where the pitiful remnant of our original freedom rises from the earth, tears apart the bonds of the flesh, and strives toward spiritual good things—there begins our heavenly birth, the adoption of the Spirit, which is received by faith.

Often we utter the name of "Our Father in heaven," but do we ever consider our right to call Him by such a name? Constantly absorbed by earthly thoughts, earthly desires, earthly actions; eagerly submitting to busyness together with the rest of creation that is subjected to it unwillingly; recklessly continuing being "flesh," as *that which is born of the flesh*—what part do we have in the heavenly Father? How can we place ourselves in the ranks of His sons together with the Only-begotten One, who is *the brightness of His glory and the express image of His person*?

When we name Him "Our Father" not in order to gratefully confess our gracious adoption, but only to flatter (if this were even possible) His mercy, do we honestly think that our moaning will disarm the righteousness of God who *triest the very hearts and reins*?[5] No! He answers the brazen invocation of the son of the world and the flesh. I am not your Father until you seek to become my child internally. *You are of your father the Devil, and the*

---

5   Readers of any Orthodox Psalter will note the discrepancy between Metropolitan Philaret's reading of this verse and the LXX version. This is likely because Russian scholars of the time preferred the Masoretic text.

desires of your father you want to do. It is appropriate that for you, I only be the Lord of slaves, the Judge of the condemned. *John 8:44*

O Christians, let us allow God to be for us that which we call Him. Let us lift ourselves up from the earth. Let us seek the heavenly fatherland. Then, without guilt, we may call Him our Father in heaven, and He, without wrath, will hear our petitions.

Hallowed be Thy name. This is our first petition. *Matthew 6:9*

God's name is the most sacred thing in the world. The salvific Mysteries are accomplished in this name. This name seals the faithfulness of our vows and promises. We place this name at the foundation of all our work. There was a time when it, being uttered by the lips of the servants of God, majestically shook the natural world and cast down enemies both visible and invisible. This ineffable power is God's own power, but its activity within us depends on our faith and piety. Therefore, we are commanded to preserve the name of God with reverence and to use it sparingly, lest you *take the name of the Lord your God in vain.* Therefore, admitting ourselves to be unworthy keepers of this heavenly treasure, we must pray our heavenly Father that His name—eternally holy in itself—be hallowed in us as well. We pray that we will utter it with grace-filled power, that we will faithfully invoke it with our deeds, that *[our] light so shine before men, that they may see [our] good works and glorify [our] Father in heaven.* *Deuteronomy 5:11*

Matthew 5:16

But what if the tongue of the praying man—he who must hallow the name of God or, rather, be sanctified by it—is not yet purified of idle talking, gossip, lying, and slander? What if the desire of our hearts battles against the desire of our lips? What if the noise of our *moliebens* and our doxologies *caused the cry of the poor* to heaven, instead of praising God, the Father of orphans? What if our prayers are drowned out by *the voice of [our] brothers' blood,* for our prayers do not praise God, the Judge of those who injure others? What benefit is there if we bear the praise of God on our tongue when the tongues of others who look at our life speak to each other in amazement: *Where is their God?* *Job 34:28*

Genesis 4:10

Psalm 78:10

As much as you can, *keep thy tongue from evil...and do good* with your whole heart. Then your prayer will not be in vain: "Hallowed be Thy name."

Thy kingdom come—this is the second petition of the sons of the kingdom.

The kingdom of God is *an everlasting kingdom*. Even before the ages, God was the king of His own hidden eternity. Now, within time, He reveals the lordship of the Creator and Provider in the kingdom of nature, and in the kingdom of the grace of the love of the Father for the Savior. So much so, that we *see* Him here, but *through a mirror, dimly*. Finally, both these kingdoms, gradually moving toward their pre-determined conclusion, will be transfigured into the one kingdom of glory, in which He will appear to the sons of the kingdom *face to face*. He will then raise them from glory to glory. Many will be surrounded by this coming kingdom, a gift of God to men, but will nevertheless be allotted to the left side. Only the chosen, those who bear within themselves the seed of the kingdom, will be called to *inherit the kingdom prepared for [them] from the foundation of the world*.

Thus, our prayer concerning the coming of the kingdom is a pious desire that God accomplish *the earnest expectation of the creation eagerly [awaiting] the revealing of the sons of God*. May God make us worthy to meet this earnest expectation, this event desired by the entire world.

Do we have such a sincere desire? We desire the kingdom of God and know that this kingdom is *not of this world*, but do not many of us create our own kingdoms of frivolous fantasy here on earth? The son of power wants his sword to sow fear and humiliation among others. The so-called wise man imagines for himself new laws of comfort and amusement. The avaricious builds a dark kingdom and gathers soulless minions in his treasure-houses. We desire the kingdom of God and believe that only the narrow gate and difficult way lead to it. However, do we not often hurry to forestall others to find a place on the wide path, to walk through broad gates? We love to place ourselves to the right of others, never imagining that, by the law of natural consequence, we are placing ourselves on the left of the Lord at His coming! We desire the kingdom of God and have heard that is it *taken by force*, but do we do anything forceful to attain it? Do we not instead pray for the coming of the kingdom only so that we may lay the burden of this great undertaking onto God's own shoulders?

Matthew 11:12

Let us grow zealous in serving God, just as we are already zealous to be a master in the world. Let us go meet the kingdom of God by the path of the Cross and humility. Then, our prayer concerning its coming will not be hypocritical.

The third petition: *Thy will be done on earth as it is in heaven.*

Our God does all that He wishes, both in heaven and on earth: for who has resisted His will? Therefore, without a doubt, it is not an increase of might that we desire for the Almighty in this petition. Man, gifted with free will, sees his only blessedness in the single will of his Creator. Therefore, he prays that God's good and complete will overcome his own incomplete and weak will, that He act in us *both to will and to do*. But what is the will of God "on earth, as it is in heaven?"

Romans 9:19

Philippians 2:13

The angels are in heaven. Man is on earth. When the earth-born will serve God with love as fiery, with zeal as unconstrained, as the angels, then God's will shall be done on earth and in heaven equally. The Church of the faithful is heaven on earth. The darkened and deluded world is only earth. When even the fallen sheep will recognize the salvific voice of the Pastor, and when those who sit in the darkness and the shadow of death will see a great light, then the will of the Father of lights will be done on earth, as it is in heaven.

The spirit is, in a certain way, heaven within man. The flesh is earth. When the inner man who *delight[s] in the law of God* will put down the *law in [his] members*, and the flesh takes its proper

Romans 7:22-23

position of submissive servant, then the will of the God of spirits will be done on earth as it is in heaven.

We speak much about the will of God, but we think of the fulfillment of our own will far more! We desire to see a heavenly earth, after the fulfillment of God's will, or a transformation of earth into heaven itself. But do we begin this great transformation within ourselves? O love of angels! You are greater than I. I do not dare seek you. O Christian love! Where do you reside? Where do you act, O pious zeal? Where do you hide, O meek submissiveness to the will of God? Instead of ascension from earth to heaven, from the Christian life to the angelic, do we not instead see within ourselves a descent from heaven to earth, a humiliation of the spirit before the flesh, a fall of the blessed kingdom of grace before the insurgent lordship of debauched nature?

Let us first come to hate our evil self-will, and then we can pray about God's good will within us.

Dear listeners, these three petitions must be offered to the Lord by us with extreme prudence and reverence, because they refer to eternal things. The next four petitions refer more to temporal cares. However, we must remember that a sensible care for the temporal can result in prosperity, while an unreasonable amount of worry for the temporal will bring down the wrath of the Eternal One upon us.

Matthew 6:11   *Give us this day our daily bread.*

This should be the limit of our cares for the good things of this earth. Life is good only because through it we can earn blessed eternity. Therefore, only that which preserves life is good for us. Whoever realizes how much he must do for eternity does not have much time to care for this temporal life. Thankfully, the good Provider removes our need to labor for the temporal as soon as we dedicate ourselves to the needs of the eternal: *But seek first the kingdom of God and His righteousness, and all these things shall be added to you.* *Matthew 6:33*

Therefore, the faithful children of God ask for what they need not from slaves, but from the Father. They do not request frivolous decorations and worthless baubles, but *bread*. Not delicious bread, but *daily*, that is, only that which is necessary for the needs of the day. They do not even ask for full granaries for a year, only today for the daily meal. *Sufficient*, they say, *for the day is its own trouble*. Why should we harass our caring Father about needs that, perhaps, will no longer exist tomorrow? But even with such limited needs, we must think not so much about the bread that fills the body, but the bread that satisfies the essential part of man, for *Man shall not live by bread alone, but by every word that proceeds from the mouth of God*. *Matthew 6:34*

Matthew 4:4

Do any of us even know how to sense the salvific voice of the Word of God, much less be satisfied by it better than bread? Is not our spiritual hunger often put down by the greed of the flesh that requires us not to be satisfied, but over-satiated? The flesh desires not clothing, but finery. It seeks not health to be able to accomplish one's work, but languor and pleasant inactivity. Having satisfied ourselves with the usual temporal needs, we invent for ourselves unforeseen disasters and requirements for our future years, none of which may ever occur. Finally, not content with insulting God with such excessive desires, we even abandon Him and turn with our needs to the powerful of the earth, to cunning, to falsehood, and in this manner, we add insolence to our faithlessness.

Let us be more moderate in our desires and more circumspect in our choice of what is necessary for us. Only prudent moderation knows how to ask bread from the *Bread of life*. *John 6:35*

And forgive us our debts, as we forgive our debtors.[6] *Matthew 6:12*

---

6   Although most English speakers will be more familiar with "trespasses" instead of "debts," the Slavonic version, and the author's Russian commentary, make more sense if we choose to use "debts."

How many debts we have before God! First of all, there is our inherited debt. Our forefather Adam bought the forbidden fruit with the cost of his life and his posterity. We were born debtors. Then, there are our own, personal debts. God invisibly hands out many precious *talents* to us, both external and internal, *each according to his ability.* To use them for good and for His glory—this is the interest he demands of us. Every iniquitous act, every perverse desire, every evil thought is counted by the Omniscience, and they comprise the horrifying cost of our debts. We cannot pay them back.

Matthew 25:15

But see what an easy arrangement God offers us in return! *If you forgive men their debts, your heavenly Father will also forgive you.* For the sake of this holy agreement, we bring with us all our debtors to lay before His gaze. We will show our mercy to His mercy, and if every single person tried in this way to wash away the evil he did before the sight of God, then the lists of our sins would gradually disappear, until finally, the mutual forgiveness of everyone and all would become a single, universal justification for mankind, to the unutterable glory of the Merciful One, to the ineffable blessedness of those pardoned.

Matthew 6:14

Some may protest at this. Would it not be just as easy for the limitless Mercy to forgive the sins and errors of us weak mortals without condition, no matter how great their number? But I answer thus. Would it not be easier for you to forgive the incomparably lesser insults of your neighbor? It is true that the mercy of God is limitless; therefore, it desires that not you only, but that all mankind receive forgiveness. And, as God gives forgiveness to you, it is as if he asks you to do the same to your brothers. O man! You who live and breathe only by the mercy of the Lord! If you reject His intercession on behalf of your brothers, how can He accept the intercession of His Son on your behalf? For in such a case, the forgiveness of our debts as we forgive our debtors contains within itself our own condemnation, *for judgment is without mercy to the one who has shown no mercy.*

James 2:13

Let us not forget, O Christians, to forgive first, before we ask for mercy. *Blessed are the merciful, for they shall obtain mercy.* *Matthew 5:7*

And lead us not into temptation. *Matthew 6:13*

Forgiveness of our sins would be useless for us if we always returned to them with the same weakness. But how difficult it is not to fall at any time during the constant war against flesh, the world, and the spirits of evil! The lion roars; the foxes lay their traps. If we use our prescience to battle evil, we fall to its superior force. If we attack anger with strength, then we are tripped up by cunning. We have not a single hope, until the moment the Victorious One will no longer allow any attacks that we cannot withstand, or until He gives us the necessary artistry and power to be completely victorious.

And we pray, dear listeners, that He preserves us from temptations. But do we not approach them ourselves, even before they attack us? We pray that the flesh does not enslave us. But do we not feed and warm this enemy of ours, serving it as a friend and even a lord? We pray that the world does not enthrall us. But do we not open our ears to its putrid charms? We pray that our eye does not tempt us. But do we not nail our eyes to earthly delights? Against whom then do we pray, if not against ourselves? *But each one is tempted when he is drawn away by his own desires and enticed.* *James 1:14*

It hinges on us, whether or not to run toward temptations. Only those temptations which we encounter against our will can be pushed aside by the words of the prayer.

But deliver us from the evil one. *Matthew 6:13*

Finally, there is a certain form of evil in our damaged nature that is found not so much in the inner essence of things as in an external manifestation, through actions and transitory sensations. It is not always the scourge of a punishing justice, but often it is a striking rod of love, bitter medicine, and, so to speak, potential good. Poverty, sickness, sorrow, humiliation, and persecution are only evils when we are at fault for them. However, our weak nature shudders even before the image of suffering. And how great is the compassion of our heavenly Father, who allows us to ask Him to give us peace even from these apparitions of evil! He allows us to ask Him to quickly disperse even these slight shadows that run along the vale of life.

And how much more impudent and ungracious are we, when we use this incredible condescension for evil! How many people cry out to God at every misfortune that their own hands crafted! The one who lost his health through intemperate living comes to complain to God about his weakness. The one whose conscience condemns him for offending others dares to invoke the judgment of God against those he has offended! The one who lived a dissolute life utters curses against his own poverty. Should such people ask the Lord to deliver them from evil? Or would it not be better for them to thank Providence for their forthcoming condemnation, and the resulting correction of their evil heart?

Dear listeners, let us joyfully bear all deserved punishments. And when we suffer as innocents, let us not rush to pray for deliverance from our misfortune. *For your heavenly Father knows that you need all these things.*

Matthew 6:32

Truly, O all-knowing Father! Thou dost not give Thy child *a stone when he asks for bread, or a serpent when he asks for a fish*. But *we do not know what we should pray for as we ought*. It does not take long for us to see the flaws in our prayers, and without Thee, we will never achieve perfection in prayer. Correct it Thyself, "as incense before Thy face." Let not our mouths alone, but our thoughts, our heart, our desires, our actions, our spirit, our body, and *all [our] bones shall say, Lord, O Lord!*

Matthew 7:9-10
Romans 8:26

Psalm 34:10

For Thine is the kingdom and the power and the glory forever. Amen

Matthew 6:13

15

On Praying with the Spirit and the Understanding (1829)

"I will pray with the spirit, and I will also pray with the understanding. I will sing with the spirit, and I will also sing with the understanding." (1 Corinthians 14:15)

Prayer is a labor of such importance in the spiritual life that if someone wanted to determine for himself whether or not he walks on the path toward perfection in the spiritual life, he need only notice whether or not he has any success with his prayer. For if we take to heart the words of the Lord, *And whatever things you ask in prayer, believing, you will receive*, then by necessity we must conclude that whoever is able with faith in prayer to ask for everything necessary for perfection in the spiritual life—that person will receive it all. Therefore, without a doubt, that is the person who walks toward perfection in the spiritual life and finally will reach it.

Matthew 21:22

Judging by this significance of prayer for the spiritual life, we must be very assiduous in practicing the best and most trustworthy method of prayer.

Let us be attentive. When the Apostle Paul expressed how he would best desire to pray himself, he thereby gave us the most trustworthy counsel concerning the best way for us to pray as well. *I will pray with the spirit, and I will pray also with the understanding. I will sing with the spirit, and I will also sing with the understanding.*

In these words of the Apostle we see, first of all, two external forms of prayer. *I will pray* and *I will sing*. These are spoken prayers and sung prayers.

Concerning these forms of prayer, it is enough to note how faithfully the holy Church follows the example and teaching of the Apostle, since to this day we encounter both reading and singing in the church services. We will also call attention to the fact that both forms of prayer are universally applicable and useful, not only for the beginner who is still led astray by physical impressions, but even for those of exalted mind, since even the divinely wise Apostle desired not only to pray with the spirit and understanding, but also to sing aloud from a heart overflowing with divine love and a spirit overcome with compunction.

Secondly, there are two other specific forms of prayer mentioned in the Epistle—the prayer of the spirit and the prayer of the understanding.

To understand these exalted forms of prayer, we must first understand what the words *spirit* and *understanding* mean in the apostolic lexicon. When we hear the Apostle saying that *those who live according to the flesh set their minds on the things of the flesh, but those who live according to the Spirit, the things of the Spirit*, then we can understand that the spirit is something exalted in man, contrary to the flesh or sensuality. And when we hear the Apostle say the following, *with the mind I myself serve the law of God, but with the flesh the law of sin*, then we can understand that the mind is also an exalted aspect of man, something contrary to the flesh. Therefore, it seems that the spirit and the understanding constitute nearly the same thing, since the Apostle unites them when describing the truth or the essence of Christian teaching, which consists of *being renewed in the spirit of your mind*. If we do note some difference between the mind and the spirit, then it is only that the spirit seems to be an exalted aspect of the mind itself, something more internal that is revealed within the mind, similarly to how the soul is revealed within the physical senses.

Ephesians 4:23

However, there are other passages in the Epistles where the activity of the mind in prayer is presented with a certain opposition to the activity of the spirit. For example, "my spirit prays, but my understanding is unfruitful." This suggests that the distinction between them is not slight at all, but quite vividly sensed. In order to better determine this distinction, I will quote the entire passage: *For if I pray in a tongue, my spirit prays, but my understanding is unfruitful. What is the conclusion then? I will pray with the spirit, and I will also pray with the understanding. I will sing with the spirit, and I will also sing with the understanding.* This makes it obvious that the expression *I will pray with the spirit* is given a place preceding the expression *I pray in a tongue*. Consequently, *the prayer of the spirit* is the same as *the prayer in a tongue*. Therefore, to understand the prayer of the spirit, we must first understand what it means to pray in a tongue.

1 Corinthians 14:14-15

Lest I exhaust you with a lengthy exegesis, I will hurry to explain the essence of this passage. When the Apostles after the Ascension *continued with one accord in prayer and supplication;* and when ten days afterward *they were all filled with the Holy Spirit and began to speak with other tongues, as the Spirit gave them utterance,* they received the gift of speaking in languages they did not previously know. It was an extremely magnificent fruit of their prayer, an extremely majestic sign of the descent of the Holy Spirit acting within them. From that moment, the prayer and eagerness of all the faithful was intended especially toward the acquisition of this specific gift of the Spirit, since it was so useful in those times of the early Christian mission. It was also a pleas-

Acts 1:14

Acts 2:4

ant gift for those who acquired it, since it was such an obvious confirmation of the presence of grace within them.

As long as this striving of the faithful corresponded to the intention of grace to spread the Christian faith, this grace came down generously to bless that striving, and so it often happened that during church gatherings, the spirit of those praying fell into ecstatic states. The Spirit of God would descend on the spirits of those praying, and, like a torrent that couldn't be held back, it poured out through the lips of those praying in the form of hymns, doxologies, and prophecies in different languages. The abundance of this gift was so great that sometimes those who were filled with the Spirit uttered divine songs in languages that the majority of attendees (or sometimes all of them) could not even understand. This is the *tongue* that the Apostle Paul speaks of in when he says, *If I pray in a tongue.* In other words, the *tongue* here refers to unknown languages that are revealed only by the gift of the Holy Spirit. In such cases, "My spirit prays, but my understanding is unfruitful." The mind is unfruitful because other people do not understand the meaning of the prayer, and so the words of this prayer, sowed by a foreign tongue, bring no spiritual fruit of prayer in the souls of others.

After this, I hope it is more understandable that *the prayer of the spirit* is a state of prayer in which a person, given wings by faith and love—by the very height of his essence, so to speak, by his highest capabilities and powers, through which he is, as it were, adjacent to the divine—strives toward, and is exalted toward, the Spirit of God. In this state, he accepts the descent of the Holy Spirit, and he abandons himself to this descent, so that it is no longer he who prays, but the Holy Spirit who breathes within him. This is the same Spirit that *blows where [He] wishes, the Spirit Himself [who] makes intercessions for us with groanings which cannot be uttered.* These prayers are utterances that often surpass the understanding of physical mankind.

John 3:8
Romans 8:26

The prayer of the understanding, which the Apostle distinguishes from the prayer of the spirit, is the kind of prayer when the mind of the one praying rises to God with pious thoughts and desires, with holy emotions of compunction and joy. However, it is not subject to the attraction of spiritual ecstasy in a limitless fashion. In other words, the person can still direct his thoughts, desires, and emotions, so that his spiritual powers act in their usual, natural manner. Therefore, prayerful petitions and doxologies uttered in this state can incite others to participation in this prayer.

The holy Apostle sanctions and offers both forms of prayer as appropriate. In other words, he does not counsel them to use only one of these forms of prayer to the exclusion of the other. He considers it best to sometimes pray in the spirit, and sometimes to pray with the understanding, depending on the circumstances. He suggests praying with the spirit for oneself and for God, while praying with the understanding is good for God, for oneself, and for the exhortation of one's neighbors.

We cannot go further without making a special point of mentioning, even with some amazement, that the Apostle offers the prayer of the spirit (which is a gift of the Spirit of God) equally with the prayer of the understanding, which is performed by the free activity of the human spirit. How is this possible? Is he saying that we are equally empowered to pray with the spirit as with the mind? Have you ever even thought about this, O holy Teacher!

Yes, without a doubt, brothers, the Holy Spirit, speaking through St. Paul, did not make a mistake with this instruction. Evidently, we truly have the authority to pray with the spirit— as soon as we truly and completely submit to the Spirit of God, who is the Spirit of prayer. Evidently, we have this authority, by the wondrous condescension of the Spirit of God, in a similar way to how the prophets had the authority to wield the spirit of prophecy, as the same Apostle also witnesses: *And the spirits of the prophets are subject to the prophets.*

> 1 Corinthians 14:32

But we should be even more amazed by the fact that the Apostle doesn't try to push or overly encourage the grace-filled prayer of the spirit, but instead he seeks to somewhat limit it and hold it within a proper striving. He even complains of the overabundant use of the prayer in the spirit. With even some distress, he speaks thus: *my spirit prays, but my understanding is unfruitful.* It's almost as though he prefers the prayer of the mind and primarily exhorts one to pray with the understanding: *Yet in the church I would rather speak five words with my understanding, that I may teach others also, than ten thousand words in a tongue.* What does that mean? It means that the grace of the Holy Spirit poured like an ocean in the early Church. Most of the faithful needed not to be exhorted to prayer, nor inspired to the deeds of the spirit, but rather their limitless zeal needed to be moderated so that they, being submerged in the spirit, did not forget the everyday duties in the life of a human being and a Christian.

> 1 Corinthians 14:14

> 1 Corinthians 14:19

If we turn from this spiritual vision of the early Church and return to its current state and to our own selves, then should we not come to a different sort of amazement, or, perhaps, should we not be seized with fear and horror, considering the shameful difference between our state and theirs? Have many of us been so overwhelmed with the prayer of the spirit that we had to be pulled out of the sea of the spirit to the shore of the understanding? Have many of us, even a little bit, ever experienced prayer in the spirit? Do we even understand what it is, when we speak of it?

Some may say, "Why are you even speaking with us about this prayer, which is so extraordinary and so inexplicable?" Let them complain, whoever wants to. But I speak of this exalted prayer exactly because it has become so extraordinary and so little understood. It is necessary for this age to know that gifts of grace that once were completely normal have now become strange. The wise men of this age must know that what is so hard for them to understand in these descriptions of states of grace used to be understood by common people who listened to the Apostle Paul or read his Epistles. Furthermore, I say to this late and dark age, that even earlier it was commanded that the Angel of the Church of Ephesus utter these words, *Remember therefore from where you have fallen; repent and do the first works.* *Revelation 2:5*

Truly, brothers, we have fallen far from the pious zeal, the spiritual progress of the first Christians when not only the wondrous prayer in the spirit has all but disappeared, but often the prayer of the understanding is inattentive, the prayer of the heart is cold, and the prayer of the lips is not inspired by the prayer of the mind and the heart.

Let us repent and emulate the first works of the first Christians. Let us force ourselves to endure in prayer and exhortation, that is, to abide in prayer constantly and without weakening, as much as this is possible. Let us stand guard over our mind and our emotions with attention, so that we will chase away our vain thoughts, passionate desires, and sensual, enticing impressions and memories from our prayer, like Abraham in ancient times chased away birds of prey from his sacrifices. Let us approach God not only with our mouths, but first and foremost with our hearts. Let us pray and sing with our understanding, with zeal, let us pray and sing finally with our spirit, according to the gift of the Holy Spirit, to whom be glory, together with the Father and the Son forever. Amen.

16

On the Rest of Those Who Labor and are Heavy Laden (1825)

"Come to Me, all you who labor and are heavy laden, and I will give you rest." (Matthew 11:28)

Listen, He is calling you! Should you heed this call? *You who labor and are heavy laden*—are there any such here? Or is it easy and not difficult for us, and so this call has nothing to do with us? He promises to "give us rest." Is there anyone here who needs rest? Or is it not worth the effort to follow Him? Maybe we just want joy, happiness, diversions?

Matthew 11:28

Let me ask the question a little differently. Do you want to be successful? Doubtless, everyone would say yes. But what would you call the spiritual state of a successful person? I think this state is best characterized by one of two possible words: peace or joy. But typical, earthly joy acts on a person like wine. A joyful state is a state of drunkenness, and not prolonged drunkenness either. It leaves behind itself a sense of loss or even heaviness. Peace is the state of a healthy and sober soul. It is not as vivid a sense as joy, but it is more constant. Thus, do not be angry with me, all you lovers of joy, merriment, and amusements. I desire (and I think is necessary for your benefit) that you have more peace in your heart than joy, merriment, and amusements.

After all, whoever has trained his taste to prefer earthly joy finds it so easily, and replaces labors with merriment so tirelessly, that he has no patience for peace. To such a person (though this may seem too harsh to some), we even desire that he experience, for a time, the state of those who "labor and are heavy laden." Despite the harshness of this desire, we actually emulate a certain extremely benevolent man, who said, *Make their faces ashamed, O Lord, and they shall seek Thy Name.* [Psalm 82:17]

However, it's possible that the state of those who labor and are heavy laden is neither rare nor foreign to many of us. In this case, we must seek rest, and we must run to the Giver of peace.

Come to Me, all you who labor and are heavy laden, [Matthew 11:28] exclaimed the Lord Jesus, when He gazed at the Jews to whom He preached. What sort of yoke could He have seen on their backs? What kind of burden weighed them down? First of all, the burden of sins, under which even the powerful king of Israel labored, like a slave afflicted with disease in the bones after a life of carrying extremely heavy weights: *Neither is there any rest in my bones, by reason of my sin. For my wickednesses are gone over my head; like a sore burden have they become too heavy for me.* [Psalm 37:4-5]

Second of all, the yoke of the law of Moses, which the Apostle Peter did actually call a yoke *which neither our fathers nor we were able to bear.* [Acts 15:10] That yoke, in the last days before Christ's coming, had been made doubly and triply heavy by the teachings and human commandments of the Scribes and Pharisees. As the Lord Himself said, *For they bind heavy burdens, hard to bear, and lay them on men's shoulders.* [Matthew 23:4]

Third of all, there were many different yokes and burdens in the form of the many calamities that lay on the Jewish people at that time and that continued to plague them afterward. For example, the yoke of the pagan authority, under which the proud

SERMON 16: ON THE REST OF THOSE WHO LABOR AND ARE HEAVY LADEN 111

Jews tried to raise their heads and cry out, *We are Abraham's descendants, and have never been in bondage to anyone.* Nevertheless, that yoke lay heavy on their necks, rising up over their heads, since it lay even on the High Priesthood and on the very robes of the high priest, for the Romans kept it under lock and key. The yoke of the synagogue also lay heavy, which persecuted those who confessed the truth that offended their prejudices and love of power. Finally, there were the private burdens of poverty, oppression by the strong, unjust rulings in court, diseases, and sorrows.

John 8:33

The Lord Jesus Christ called all these, and similarly burdened people, to Himself. And since He called all without exception; since God the Father sent Him *as Savior of the world*, not to a single nation or time; since His words *will by no means pass away* even when *heaven and earth will pass away*—then even now He is still saying these words, calling those who labor and are heavy laden among us. He calls us to Himself.

1 John 4:14

Mark 13:31

O man, you who know your own sin! Do you not labor? Are you not heavy laden? Do you not feel the wound on your conscience? Do you not seek to run away from yourself, though the effort is in vain, just like a wounded deer who tries to run through the woods, but only loses its strength in the process? Is not your sin often your burden, since it weighs down your soul with remembrance of the evil you committed? Is not your sin often your yoke, since it deprives you of freedom, just like a beast of burden is tied down, belabored, and exhausted by a physical yoke? If you still live in sin and do not know or sense that it is a burden and a yoke, that is no better. In this case, you are like a wild, yoked animal that rushes along the edge of a cliff. The less it feels the pull of its burden, the less it is hindered, the faster it falls into the abyss and is lost.

Therefore, in this case (as we have already said) it is better if you begin to sense the unpleasant state of those who labor and are heavy laden, rather than remain in the dangerous state of being unbridled. However, you who know your own sins to be a burden and a yoke, you must hurry to know also the hope of relief. "Come to me, you who labor and are heavy laden."

O man! You who labor in virtue. Do you not also labor? Are you not also heavy laden? Yes, it is true that if the fate of the sinner is a yoke and a burden, then the fate of virtue must be lightness and freedom. But just as the yoke and burden of sin is sensed only after the sin is committed, so also virtue only imparts lightness and freedom after it has been accomplished. But is the process of accomplishing perfection in virtue easy? No. That road leads into the mountains. It is steep, narrow, and covered in thorns. Coming to know the path of spiritual perfection and actually ascending it are both difficult, if only for the reason given by a certain experienced laborer in wisdom and virtue: *For a corruptible body weighs down the soul, and this earthly tent burdens a heart full of thoughts.*

Wis. of Sol. 9:15

The body is perishable, and therefore cannot bear the full tension of an immortal soul. Instead, the body either pulls back at the soul's forward motion or runs the risk of rejecting it completely and being destroyed. Moreover, it is infected with sin and bound by habits that run contrary to virtue. As for the mind, not only is it distracted by cares for its earthly home (that is, the body), but it is also bound with prejudices, darkened and led astray by passions of the heart, and deluded by phantoms of the emotions and imagination.

And how many more obstacles there are to laboring in virtue! We are seduced by excesses of earthly good things. We are tempted by their lack. We are led from the path by the example of others. Stumbling blocks are laid down by people's incorrect judgments. Persecutions scare us. Wherever the battle "against flesh and blood" ends, there begins the war *against principalities, against powers, against the rulers of the darkness of this age, against spiritual hosts of wickedness in the heavenly places.* Whoever labors

Ephesians 6:12

not only to win a crown of accolades for virtue from people, but also to secure the true, internal victory over the passions and vices, understands the complaints that we hear from the mouth of one of the most zealous ascetics of all time: *For I know that in me (that is, in my flesh) nothing good dwells; for to will is present with me, but how to perform what is good I do not find. The good that I will to do, I do not do; but the evil I will not to do, that I practice....I find then a law, that evil is present with me, the one who wills to do good....O wretched man that I am!* O you, for whom the very law of good is a burden on the back of a paralyzed man, you must understand that you need hope, relief, or strengthening. And so *come, you who labor and are heavy laden.* *Romans 7:18-24*

Matthew 11:28

O man! You who have been visited by calamity, suffering, or sorrow. I do not need to ask if you are, or if you consider yourself to be, one of those who labor and are heavy laden. I need not worry that you lack this knowledge; rather, I worry that you feel it too strongly. I worry that through the excess of this sense, you prevent yourself from knowing the means for attaining rest and peace. The only true means is the one that reveals itself to you. Gather the scraps of your scattered strength; approach, so that you can understand and accept these words: *Come, you who labor and are heavy laden.* *Matthew 11:28*

Come to me, you who labor and are heavy laden, says Jesus Christ, *and I will give you rest.* What a trustworthy refuge! What a safe haven! What all-powerful aid! What all-conquering protection! What heavenly relief! What divine peace! Only come. Only do not reject. *Matthew 11:28*

Jesus Christ gives rest to all who labor under the yoke of the law, for even if the sins of the entire world lay on you, He will lift this burden off your shoulders and lay it on Himself, destroying it in the process. *Behold the Lamb of God that takes away the sin of the world.* If you are defeated by sin, the Lamb of God will defeat the sin inside you. If you are sold into slavery to sin, He will redeem you. If you are tied by sin as by a yoke, He will release you. If *John 1:29* you stumble under the burden of sin, He will raise you up. Even if you have been killed by sin, God who resurrected Christ will make you *alive together with Christ. The blood of Christ, who through the eternal Spirit offered Himself without spot to God, [will] cleanse your conscience from dead works to serve the living God.*

Jesus Christ gives rest to all who labor under the yoke of the law, especially those who labor in virtue, and yet experience the heaviness of the labor and the obstacles along the way more greatly than its successful resolution. Such people seem to wilt under the pressure of the labor instead of growing stronger. But Christ, the Power and Wisdom of God, gives them the light of pure knowledge, the power to complete their labor, relief from their labor and burden, removal of all obstacles, and strength for the laborer. He sends help and leads us through all dangers. He defeats our enemies, and Himself crowns us with victory. The same ascetic who only recently cried out in exhaustion and desperation, "O wretched man that I am!" approaches Christ, and then finds within himself no other feeling except gratitude to Him for His peace: *I thank God—through Jesus Christ our Lord!* To the one who labors together with Christ, *His commandments are not burdensome.* For *[His] yoke is easy and [His] burden is light.* Even the most powerless can say, when he is together with Him, *I can do all things through Christ who strengthens me.*

Jesus Christ gives relief and peace to the unfortunate, the suffering, and the sorrowful. For not only can He, as the Redeemer, always turn aside or cut off all misfortune, stop suffering, and destroy the source of sorrow; but He, as the total Victor over evil, establishes His kingdom of good in the very domain of evil. He can uncover within man a sense of well-being even in the midst of calamity. He can dissolve suffering in pleasure. He can even give sorrow the taste of joy. This is how Job, after the accidental death of his children and the loss of his wealth, praised God. Even while suffering from an unbearable disease, sitting on a dung heap, he would not agree to blame God. This is how Peter, chained in the prison, sang hymns all night as though it were a feast. This is how Paul rejoiced in his sufferings. This is how Cyprian, when hearing his death sentence, answered, "Glory to God!"

O Christian, this is truly that blessed rest given to your soul, heavenly even on this earth, deathless even before death. And it is only found in Christ. We must seek Him, but even if our own need does not bring us to our senses, then our all-good and all-merciful Savior will Himself come and call all of us to receive the rest that He gives freely.   *Matthew 11:29*

One can say that we have already been led—and are constantly being led—to this rest for our souls in Christ. We are led to Him by baptism, and every time that we approach Him in prayer, in repentance, in the communion of His body and blood. Well? Have we tasted this peace? Have we preserved it, and do we preserve its power within us? Or are we again restless, do we again labor, and are we again heavy laden? How much longer? Will it come to this, that Christ who vainly called for us so long will finally abandon us who do not listen, who remain inconstant? Will not hell—whom we serve in our busyness, being heavy laden by sin—then approach us instead? It will say: you have served me enough and carried my burdens enough. Now come, and I will give you the rest that I know. I will lay you down on the fire that does not dissipate, and I will cover you with the worm that does not die.

Let us rather, brethren, follow the gracious call of Christ. Let us cease putting it off. Let us follow Him resolutely. Let us cease turning back. I say this together with the Apostle: *Since a promise remains of entering His rest, let us fear lest any of you seem to have come short of it. Today,* said the Holy Spirit through the mouth of David, *Today,* said the Holy Spirit centuries later through Paul. And how wondrous is God's longsuffering that we still have a chance in our own time to say, *Today, if you will hear His voice, do not harden your hearts...*   *Hebrews 4:1*

Hebrews 3:7-8

Let us approach Christ from this moment with zeal and with unswerving emulation of His teaching and life. Let us enter the rest of those who believed in Him with ardent faith, with living and active faith, preceded by those ascetics of faith and virtue who have lived from time immemorial, those true followers of Jesus Christ who have already found heavenly rest from their earthly labors and burdens. They invite us to follow their example, so that together with them, we may glorify the One Giver of rest and *Savior of all men, especially of those who believe*. Amen.

1 Timothy 4:10

17

On the Easy Yoke of Christ (1828)

"For My yoke is easy, and My burden is light." (Matthew 11:30)

The Lord Jesus calls to Himself all who labor and are heavy laden, and He promises them spiritual consolation. *Come to Me, all you who labor and are heavy laden, and I will give you rest...and you will find rest for your souls.* What a pleasant call! What a longed-for promise! But what means will He use to give rest to those who labor, to give consolation to those who are heavy laden? Will He take off the yoke that oppresses them? Will He deliver them from the labors that exhausted them? Without a doubt, He will do this. However, in the first instance, He has an entirely different intention. He wants us to take upon ourselves a new yoke: *Take my yoke upon you.*

Matthew 11:28-29

Matthew 11:29

O merciful Lord! Are You sending the oppressed to yet a new labor? Are You laying on yet another yoke on the heavy-laden? Are these Your means to give us rest?

Do not be distressed. The Lord knows what He is doing, and His means, which are incompatible with our so-called wisdom, are compatible with the intention of His wisdom. Those who are oppressed by the works of the flesh and the world will find comfort if they accept a new, spiritual labor. Those who are bent low by the yoke of the Devil, bound by evil habits, oppressed in their consciences by sins, tortured and beaten down by the whips of their passions—they will find comfort and freedom only if they bow their necks under the yoke of Christ, *for My yoke is easy, and My burden is light.*

Matthew 11:30

Christians! When Jesus Christ Himself, who is the eternal Word and the eternal Truth, found it necessary to say that His yoke is easy, and His burden is light, then this, first of all, convinces us that the teaching of the Christian life, to the fulfillment of which we are called, truly is salutary and easy to accomplish. Secondly, it shows that we must confirm all those who approach to labor in the Lord that the teaching of Christianity is easy to accomplish.

Even today, we hear the complaint that our divine Teacher and the Savior of our souls had to answer such a long time ago. We hear complaints that His yoke is heavy, that His teaching is severe, that His commandments are difficult to accomplish. On what is this base complaint founded? What is the supposed difficulty? Without a doubt, it is the fact that the teaching of Christ commands a person to go against certain natural inclinations, to overcome them, to mortify them, to offer them as a sacrifice. Yes, it requires a strict purification of a Christian, not only of the external, but also the internal actions and movements, not only of deeds and words, but also of desires and thoughts. Let us break down these human accusations against divine Truth.

Truth does not hide the fact that He gives people commandments that are not as trivial as children's toys, but as heavy as the yoke that weighs down cattle. *Take My yoke.* Those who complain against the Truth must be content with this sincere admission of the truth. However, how much more revealing is Truth's admission that the commandments are the yoke; how much more

Matthew 11:29

convinced, therefore, should we be that this yoke is easy, and that this burden is light. *For My yoke is easy, and My burden is light.*   *Matthew 11:30*

People of even limited intelligence, who are not completely base in their desires, of course will not dare to demand that they be allowed to remain children forever, to play with their toys eternally. But if you desire to rise above this state, then you must pass on to pertinent work, to labors, to asceticism. You must take His yoke.

But why a yoke? the insubordinate will say. Man is not slavish cattle. Man is gifted with reason. Why not lead man from a state of childhood to a mature state by the paths of reason, using rules easily understood by the mind, easily accomplished by the will, even pleasant to the senses? Why must we be oppressed with a yoke, by rules often incomprehensible to the human mind, difficult for the human will, and unpleasant to the senses?

Very well, O wise venerators of human reason. Reveal to me these simple, easy, and pleasant rules, through which a person can easily, as though in play, win for himself perfection and prosperity. Only I fear that these rules will actually be too easy, even—to express myself clearly—frivolous. For, contrary to this self-assured human reason, undeniable experience proves that in this earthly life no ability will ever develop, no knowledge will ever be gained, no success will ever be achieved, without a person hitching himself up to some kind of yoke, without a person bearing some kind of burden. To teach a child to read, do you not have to hitch him up to the cruel yoke of school hours? Do you not oppress him with the burden of incomprehensible books? Do you not force him to repeat incoherent and unpleasant letters the entire day? And what about the higher education of this same human reason, which would prefer to be a law-giver of easy morality?

Does not a man bow under the yoke of teachers to become worthy of his name? Does he not strain to lift the burden of learning, gathered over many centuries? And, to carry that burden, does he not torture his body with wakefulness, does he not oppress his head with intense contemplation? To become rich, does not a person deny himself luxuries for a long time? Does he not bind himself with the severe law of thrift? To receive a good harvest, does not the farmer join himself to his cattle's yoke? Do not the reapers bow their backs before the small sheaf of wheat before it can serve to become their food? How much artistry, how many different labors, how many diverse tools are needed, only to make clothing to cover and protect the human body from changes in weather!

This is what human experience tells us! How then do people, who by their nature think themselves smarter and more powerful than Nature, expect to instruct themselves in virtue with less labor than learning how to read? Is it easier to make man perfect spiritually than to make him educated in a worldly sense? Is it easier to give a person eternal blessedness than to acquire perishable riches? Is it easier to acquire living food for the eternal soul than to prepare a dead repast for the mortal body? Is it easier to sew a robe of righteousness and glory not made by hands than to make the clothing of need and shame with one's own hands?

If the witness of Nature is not enough for people who prefer to listen to Nature rather than the Gospel, I will be even braver. I will reference the witness of these same people that it is not ease and pleasure, but difficulty and sacrifice that mark a truly exalted virtue or perfection in a human being. Let these people, who despise Christian asceticism only because it is difficult, let them tell me this. Are they amazed at deeds that require absolutely no difficulty to accomplish, that require no victory over the self, no self-sacrifice? When a rich man doesn't steal or take bribes—is this a great deed? Is it not a much greater thing if a person who does not have his daily bread refuses to acquire it through falsehood? When an insulted man seeks revenge—what's significant in this? Beasts do the same. But when he spares the enemy that

SERMON 17: ON THE EASY YOKE OF CHRIST

is brought low before his feet—then not only lovers of wisdom, but even casual observers agree that the victory over one's own anger is greater than victory over one's enemies. What is it that society so values in military sacrifices and in death for the Fatherland, if not the sacrifice of one's own safety for the sake of the safety of one's Fatherland?

Thus, if such virtues require labor and sacrifice to be worthy of the notice of the world and society's good opinion, then can we require anything less of virtue, if it be worthy of God and His righteous judgments? And if the need for labor and the law of sacrifice do not make social virtues impossible to accomplish, then why do you consider Christian virtue impossible only because it has the same need for labor and the same laws of sacrifice?

However, I will more directly answer why Jesus Christ lays on His followers this yoke and burden, and why this yoke is indeed good and this burden is indeed light. Let those who know and accept the witness of the Holy Scriptures remember that *man, being in honor, understood...not* the superiority of his angelic state in Paradise. Instead, deluded by the enticement of the tempter, he willingly *shall be compared unto the brute beasts, and is becoming like unto them.* This is because he has cleaved to his sensual nature, preferring it to the spiritual nature. Both by natural consequence and by righteous punishment for this iniquity, man naturally finds himself under the yoke of sensuality, so that any attempt to make this yoke of the flesh pleasant only crushes his spirit. However, all efforts to tear oneself away from this yoke any other way only end up oppressing him even more, since the crude yoke has been firmly laid on his neck. It has even become ingrown, and he, like yoked cattle, has no means of freeing himself of it. In this manner, man, according to the expression of the Apostle, is *by nature [a child] of wrath,* laboring constantly without rest, being heavy laden constantly without lessening of the burden.

Psalm 49:20

Psalm 48:13

Ephesians 2:3

This is the state in which Christ finds man, and—notice how uselessly the one who is burdened and heavy laden murmurs against the One who gives him rest—He does not yoke him who was previously unyoked. Rather, He only changed his yoke—an evil, heavy yoke for an easy and light one, the yoke of desires and passions for the yoke of salvific commandments. Truly, Christ's commandments are a yoke, for our cattle-like desires must be reined in; our bestial passions must be cut off. We should even go as far as to kill the pleasures of our flesh and bring them, like a sacrificial lamb, to the altar of the spiritual law. However, the yoke of Christ's commandments is an "easy yoke," because he who finds himself under this yoke is led from a more or less bestial state to a truly human, angelic, and even god-like state. It is a "light burden," because the Lord, who lays it on you, at the same time gives the gracious strength to bear it. The yoke of Christ is good, and His burden is light, because the more eagerly a man bears it, the more he becomes good. And the more he becomes good, the easier it becomes for him to fulfill the good commandments. Until finally, he fulfills the will of the Lord with even greater ease and pleasure than fulfilling his own. Thus, the yoke on his shoulders eventually disappears, or even transforms into wings that constantly bear him upward toward heaven.

These contemplations are enough of a justification of the truth of Christianity, enough of an argument against the accusation of strictness and severity. Truly, the severity of the commandments of Christ condemns all idle words, all unchaste glances, all impure desires, all vain thoughts. But how else can it be, when *the imagination of man's heart is evil from his youth*, while the intention of Christ is to raise this man to God, whom no evil, and no impurity, no vanity can approach?

Genesis 8:21

Whoever desires that the law of Christ would tolerate the disorderly wanderings of human desires and thoughts should be asked whether he agrees that this law of tolerance should govern the way his children or his friends relate to him? Would the father be pleased to know that his son, visibly respectful, in secret thirsted after his inheritance, eagerly expecting the day he would receive it? What friend would be happy with the gentle words and favors of his friends if he found out that in that friend's heart there was no love or faithfulness behind the empty mask of his words and caresses? If man—who cannot see the thoughts or know the desires of his neighbor—is unhappy when he senses his neighbor's unfriendliness, then how much more is it necessary for God to require man to have pure desires and thoughts, when He knows all hearts and thoughts?

In fact, the strictness of evangelical morality is not severe or cruel, and its requirements, with the help of grace given to each in measure, are easily accomplished. We, the new followers of Christ, are convinced of this by the blessed experience, confirmed by the ages, of His perfected disciples, many of whom, of course, vividly sensed the grace-filled lightness of the burden. These not only bore the complete yoke of the required commandments, but they willingly added to it the yoke of the recommended counsels of the Gospel. They not only rejected acquisition of wealth, but they rejected acquisition itself. They not only denied their flesh the pleasure it desired, but they limited the body's natural requirements, all the better to prosper in the domain of the spirit.

O you glorified yoke-bearers of Christ who have found their rest! By the examples, teachings, prayers that you have left us, help us who labor and are heavy laden with the burdens of the flesh and the world to accept with faith, and to bear with love, the easy yoke of Christ. May we find rest for our souls in this yoke. Amen.

18

On the Parable of the Tares (1825)

"Sir, did you not sow good seed in your field? How then does it have tares?" (Matthew 13:27)

I would like to say something to you, guided by the Gospel parable of the tares. Let us invoke the aid of our heavenly Sower of good seed, lest tares be planted in your hearts through my words. Instead, let good seeds be found in the worthless tares of my words, seeds that will be capable of sprouting in the soft soil of obedient hearts and bringing forth fruit for eternal life.

But perhaps someone may think, "Why are we speaking of tares in the first place?" Shouldn't the one called to sow good seeds pay all his attention to his sowing, and not pay attention to useless tares? Yes, I would like to act in this way. Let not *my mouth...speak of men's works!* If only I could avoid speaking of men's works, so vain and fatal, instead speaking only of God's deeds, so good and salvific! I dare to assume that even the Creator Himself, the One who told the parable in the first place, did not desire to speak about tares. But what is to be done? If there is danger that even when good seed is sown, tares will sprout forth; if after the wheat has already grown the tares truly do appear—

Psalm 16:4

how can we not speak of the tares? How can we not think about what to do with them?

The slaves in the parable, ignorant of the mysteries of heavenly agriculture, wanted to immediately pull out, cut off, and destroy the tares. However, the Wise Master did not allow this. *No, lest while you gather up the tares you also uproot the wheat with them.* — Matthew 13:29

But what can we do to prevent the tares from taking over and choking the good wheat? This is what I hope to speak about by examining what are the tares and how they appeared in the field.

"Sir, did you not sow good seed in your field? How then does it have tares?" What are tares? The Creator Himself answers this question in His own exegesis of the parable: "the tares are the sons of the wicked one." In this explanation, it is not difficult to notice—and we must notice it for our further illumination—that the tares refer to some people who no longer have human nature. Likewise, *the good seeds are the sons of the kingdom*; therefore, they also do not refer to human nature. In their nature, all men first of all are born from God the Creator, then secondarily from their human parents. In life, they divide into good seeds and tares. They become sons of the kingdom or sons of the wicked one. *He who sows the good seed* did not plant a new generation of seeds on the earth. Rather, in that generation that He found on the earth, he sowed sons of the kingdom and spread them over all the generations of the world. — Matthew 13:38 / Matthew 13:37

Therefore, we must conclude that the good seed indicates the spirit and particularity of being sons of the kingdom. This is why it is said, in the explanation of another parable, that *the seed is the word of God*, inasmuch as the word of God produces in men the spirit, and particularity of the sons of the kingdom. Therefore, the opposite is also true. The tares indicate the spirit and particularities of the sons of the wicked in certain people. The development of the good spiritual seed in man is the truth of faith, the good of love, the power of hope, pure thoughts, blameless desires, a sensible word, a righteous and holy deed, a spiri- — Luke 8:11

tual, heavenly, angelic, and Christian life. On the contrary, the sprouting of spiritual tares is the falsehood of faithlessness or superstition, the evil of lack of love, the false power of self-assuredness or the powerlessness of despair, an impure thought, a blameworthy desire, a false or unchaste word, an unrighteous or wicked deed, and a carnal, earthly, bestial, hellish, in a single word—an un-Christian life.

"Sir, did You not sow good seed in your field?" You sowed on the earth that which you brought with You from the heavens: the spirit of God, the qualities of heaven. Your field is the hearts of the chosen people. You planted within them the seed of the word of God. You warmed that seed in them through the warmth of the Holy Spirit. You nurtured it through Your divine blood. It sprouted and flowered and brought forth fruit to eternal life, *some a hundredfold, some sixty, some thirty*, in the apostles, the martyrs, and in all the different kinds of saints. Through them, countries, nations, and ages have been sowed as well. More than all this, in order to preserve Your seed always pure and inexhaustible, You commanded, *Fill an omer with it, to be kept for your generations.* In other words, You have filled a certain measure of the Holy Scriptures with the word of God, so that only a few pieces of bread would feed thousands of hungry men, and yet the bread would not diminish, but only increase. In a similar way, from the small number of divine books thousands upon thousands have been taught, but the mysteries and the explanations of the mysteries of Your wisdom do not diminish, but only constantly increase.

Matthew 13:23

O Lord! What good seed this is! And with what wise care for its goodness and purity did You sow it in Your field!

"How then did it have tares?" How can Your field, O Lord, have tares? If they appeared in a place where nothing was sown, or if the evil weed arose where it had been planted, there would be nothing to wonder at. If there are delusions and vices among the pagans, what more can you expect of such wild and uncultivated land? But how did the tares of paganism appear on the field of

Christianity, which was cultivated by the cross of the God-Man, sowed by the Word of God? From where did the errors of your minds appear, O disciples of the Word of God? From where did the vices of your heart arise, fosterlings of the Holy Spirit?

To such difficult, but useful questions, we have easy, yet very dangerous answers. We say that our errors are due to human limitation. Our vices come from human weakness. What a wonderful genealogy of errors and vices! Wonderful to be used by people who are committed to their errors and who wallow in their vices—people whom the parable calls "sons of the wicked one"—to convince themselves and others that they are not of an evil generation! There is no fault in being limited. It is not shameful to admit to human weakness. But from this, they conclude that to be superstitious or to be lacking in faith entirely is a guiltless deed. Therefore, to persist in vices is also not shameful.

Error due to limitation? Is it completely true that limitation gives birth to error? Limitation is sterile. It gives birth to nothing, for it in itself is also not anything at all. It is merely a border, an edge, a deficiency of essence. Let us take, for example, the ability to see. Your eye is limited. For this reason, you cease seeing certain objects if they are removed to a great distance, and that is all. But if your eye leads you into error, imagining the objects surrounding you to be spinning about or falling in ways that they are not, then you should look for the source of your vertigo in hallucinogenic plants or in your excessive consumption of wine (not in your eye).

The same is true of the spiritual sight of the mind. Your mind is limited. For this reason, knowledge that is distant from your mental sight is therefore unknown or inexplicable. Nothing more. However, if you want to turn the entire cosmos upside down because of your ideas, then all you are doing is descending into stupidity. Can you excuse it with your limitation, which is not an active principle, and which belongs to all mankind equally? Should you not, instead, admit that your errors come from being drunk on impure and spoiled wine or the stupefying herbs of the kind of "wisdom" that, though it calls itself earthly and human, comes from a source far worse than anything purely earthly, its root being far baser than human nature?

Vices from weakness! In other words, to be virtuous, you have to be as powerful as a giant! And yet we know the contrary to be true from Scripture. For when "there were giants on the earth," then "the wickedness of man was great in the earth." (Genesis 6:4-5) So in our own time we often see that people who boast in their strength of spirit and who have fewer reasons than others to complain of physical weakness or limitation fall prey to vices more often than those who are stricken with physical weakness and limitation and who ascribe no spiritual strength to themselves at all.

Vices from weakness! On the contrary! Even a pagan noticed that "we become better when we are weaker." Vices from weakness! We will agree that even this happens in some cases. For example, when a hungry pauper steals a piece of bread from a rich man. But then we see that the rich man not only refuses to give the poor man bread, but robs and ruins the poor! And we also see that there are poor people who completely lack avarice. How can you explain this with human weakness alone? Do you not see that there are two opposing powers here? In one, there is the power of good that can be greater than human, while in the other there is a power of evil that is, without a doubt, far worse than human.

Let us stop deluding ourselves. Let us lay aside these opinions concerning the source of our errors and vices, for we are capable only of increasing our errors and vices. Let us not consider a tare to be a normal plant, a natural companion to wheat. And if you cannot guess where they come from truly, then let us ask the Lord about this, and let us receive His wisdom on the matter: "Sir, did you not sow good seed in your field? How then does it have tares?" He answers. *"An enemy has done this.' While men slept, his enemy came and sowed tares among the wheat and went his way. 'The enemy who sowed them is the devil.'* *Matthew 13:28, 25,*

It seems to me that if we thought about this source for the tares in our soul more often and with greater faith, then we would not allow them to irritate us and to grow so wildly. "The enemy who sowed them is the devil." He sowed them through frivolous or evil books, through effeminate songs, through tempting spectacles, through self-will, through our un-chaste and inconstant manner of living. This is where the enemy hides: *his enemy came and sowed tares among the wheat and went his way.* *Matthew 13:25* Do you think that the pleasures of sight, hearing, imagination, and the senses that you allow yourselves are innocent? But be attentive! Through even such innocent pleasures the tares of the evil one are sown. The seed of hell roots itself in our hearts. You should feel revulsion! Be afraid and take care.

Be careful, for the parable says that *while men slept, his enemy came.* What exactly is this sleep? The Creator does not explain. *Matthew 13:25* However, we can guess, without fearing error, that the sleep in this case is man's lack of attentive care for himself and his own actions. People sleep spiritually when they close the eyes of their mind and do not try to look at the light of the truth of the Gospel and the law of God, when they cease to illumine the paths of their life constantly with that light. As if living in a dreamworld, they do not direct their thoughts or rein in their desires. They allow their imagination to wander and fix itself on sensual and vain objects. And so they sleep, but the enemy does not sleep. He creeps in the darkness of forgetfulness of God and His law, and he plants tares among the wheat. During physical sleep, he inspires hellish images. During frivolous laziness concerning one's virtue and salvation, he plants impure thoughts, sinful desires, and lawless and deadly deeds. Do not sleep! Wake up, beloved soul. Open your eyes to the light of God. Walk in the presence of God. Be attentive not only to your deeds, but even to your desires and thoughts. Be illumined within by the word of God and prayer, so that during your physical sleep, the dawn of the spirit will not fade in your heart, and will not allow the dark enemy to approach, sowing his tares.

Sons of the kingdom, in whom the good seed is sown! The parable says that the tares become more obvious with the increased growth and ripening of the wheat. The nearer the harvest, the worse the tares. Truly, how obvious are the tares in the field of the Lord! Is this not also because the great harvest is near? For truly, it is said, *First gather together the tares and bind them in bundles to burn them.* The tares are beginning to prepare themselves for the final binding for burning. These are people who abandon themselves to iniquity and lawlessness individually, then from time to time unite into organizations and congregations of iniquity. Let us not sleep, brothers, but let us be vigilant! Let us preserve and nourish, each in his own heart, the seed of the Spirit, which the divine Sower sowed in us by baptism and through the instruction of the Gospel.

Matthew 13:30

As for you, O heavenly reapers, angels of God! Before you appear before us in the sound of the trumpet to announce the long-awaited and terrifying harvest, speak to us with the quiet voice of meek awakening to repentance and spiritual vigilance, *lest we sleep unto death in sin.* Stand guard around us, deliver us from the enemy who sows tares among us—tares which will feed the fire of Gehenna. Amen.

Psalm 13:3

19

On Stumbling Blocks (1840)

"Therefore let us not judge one another anymore, but rather resolve this, not to put a stumbling block or cause to fall in our brother's way." (Romans 14:13)

In the life of our Father among the saints Sergius of Radonezh, we find that he, during the time he was abbot, once heard words of ambition coming from the mouth of his own brother Stephen. "Who is Abbot in this place?" he complained. "Did I not come to this place first?" St. Sergius immediately left the monastery to live in a different isolated and secret place. The endurance, meekness, and humility of the saint are obvious in this event. But there is something confusing about this—why did he not rebuke his brother, as is his responsibility as an abbot? Why, because of one person, did he leave his entire brotherhood and service into which he had been appointed by the ecclesiastical authorities?

There are saints of a special path, before whom all must bow down in reverence, since they are directed by a special grace of God. Their actions are always justified in their consequences. However, not everyone has the right to emulate such a path, because it would be brazen if everyone began to ascribe to himself that same kind of grace. Here is an example of what I mean.

If a father has a son, or a leader has a subordinate, who acts out of line, be careful not to remain silent, leaving him without a rebuke and a word of correction. Remember God's terrifying punishment and warning to the sons of Eli, whom God punished for their lack of reverence. *I announced to [Eli] that I will judge his house forever for the iniquity of his sons.* If any kind of temptations or dissatisfaction leads you to want to leave the place you have been assigned by lawful authority, be careful. It can happen that you will bear the punishment of your self-will. You will not be able to run away from the evil of traveling the path of self-will, and you will never be able to catch that peace that you seek.

1 Kingdoms 3:13

But if St. Sergius did not act according to these usual laws that I have just described, then by what laws did he act? For a holy man must act according to holy commandments. We will understand this better if we apply to his action this rule of the Apostle: *Rather resolve this, not to put a stumbling block or cause to fall in our brother's way.* The clairvoyant Sergius saw that it would not be proper to openly rebuke the ambitious one, because in this case a rebuke would have seemed a squabble for power, a personal vendetta between the abbot and one older than he (not to mention his own brother!). Such a rebuke would not have passed without serious stumbling blocks for the rest of the brothers of the monastery.

Romans 14:13

In this difficult situation, the wise Sergius found a way not only to avoid causing his brothers to fall, but to remove the stumbling block placed in the road by his brother. He told no one of his brother's action, and by his departure from the monastery, he offered his brother a powerful medicine against the passion of ambition. God, who directed the path of His righteous one, through his willing exile, only confirmed the love of the monks for their abbot. Subsequently, Metropolitan Alexei reinstated him, to the joy of all.

This is a vivid example of the importance of the apostolic rule: *Not to put a stumbling block or cause to fall in our brother's way*. May this holy example inspire in us an active emulation in our own life. *Romans 14:13*

But what is *a stumbling block*? What does it mean to *cause a fall in our brother's way*? If you are walking on the road, and your foot hits a stone unexpectedly, your walking motion is interrupted and you are in danger of falling. That is a stumbling block, so to speak. The Apostle uses this visual image as a metaphor for the spiritual life. Of course, he is not speaking of literally tripping while walking, but rather about obstacles in the moral and spiritual life. Moreover, he differentiates the *stumbling block* from "causing a fall." Doubtless, the latter is something worse, for it causes not merely a stumble, but a fall. We trip up in our thoughts, but we fall in our actions. We trip up in our doubts, false reasonings, confusion of thoughts, and emotional disorderliness. We fall when we sin, when we commit lawless acts. If we speak or act in such a way that our neighbor begins to have evil thoughts and spiritual disorder, then we are laying a stumbling block before him. If our words or actions give him cause, incitement, or encouragement to sin, then we are causing him to fall. Thus, this parabolic explanation of the apostle's exhortation means that we must be very attentive to prevent either our words or our actions from giving the slightest reason, incitement, or encouragement to evil thoughts, spiritual disorder, movement of passions, or, finally, the sin itself. *Romans 14:13*

To more exactly illumine this teaching, we will differentiate between the different ways we can cause our brother to stumble. These can be not only sinful acts, but even permissible ones, and sometimes even holy ones.

Is it possible, you ask, for holy actions to be a "cause for our brother to fall?" Doubtless, they can. The unerring word of God bears witness to this. What can be holier than to preach to people the salvific teaching of Christ Crucified? But this was a cause for the fall of some people, as the Apostle Paul himself said, *We preach Christ crucified, to the Jews a stumbling block and to the Greeks foolishness.* This stumbling block is not the fault of the preachers, whose work was holy, but rather the fault of those stumbling, whose carnal mindset, pride, and lack of faith derived only a source of temptation from the salvific teaching of Christ. This is similar to how a spider produces poison while eating the same nectar that produces honey in bees.

1 Corinthians 1:23

This example makes it easy to deduce a principle concerning such stumbling blocks. If the Apostles, fearing to cause the Jews to fall, had not preached Christ Crucified, then the world would never have heard His salvific teaching, and it would not have been saved. Thus it is obvious that they had to do their work, which brought salvation to the world, and not change their approach especially for people who cause themselves to stumble, who destroy themselves.

The stumbling block of the Cross is not a thing of the past, my brothers! Even today, the children of the world and the flesh are offended at the sight of powerful striving to do the deeds of the spirit and to acquire the mind of Christ Crucified. The Apostle Paul's words about not causing a brother's fall do not apply here. Let us freely do the works of holiness and salvation. The flesh does not stand trial over the spirit. The world does not legislate the work of God.

As for whether a permissible act can be a cause for a brother's fall, this we know from the following words of Apostle Paul: *But food does not commend us to God; for neither if we eat are we the better, nor if we do not eat are we the worse.* There is no need to endlessly argue about what sort of eating Paul referred to here. It is clear enough that the Apostle speaks here about the act of eating as something that is morally neutral. It has no special dignity, nor is it especially culpable before God. Therefore it is, by definition, a "permissible act." And concerning such permissible acts, Paul

1 Corinthians 8:8

speaks later, *If food makes my brother stumble, I will never again eat meat, lest I make my brother stumble.* 1 Corinthians 8:13

In these words, we find a special guideline concerning this manner of stumbling block. *I will never again eat meat, lest I make my brother stumble.* What an amazing combination of powerful exhortation and meekness! How strict was St. Paul to himself, when he forbade himself an innocent action forever, lest he cause his brother to stumble once! And how powerfully this strictness toward himself incites others to extreme care to avoid any such stumbling block! And at the same time, how great is his pastoral condescension, when he does not command anyone not to eat meat forever, but turns the severity of the interdict on himself! To others he leaves the choice whether or not to follow his example, as much as they are able. 1 Corinthians 8:13

That sinful actions are stumbling blocks needs no explanation. However, due to our lack of attentiveness, perhaps it would not be excessive to note how all sins are usually accompanied by a stumbling block for others. Through this, the sin grows exponentially. How long sometimes is the chain, how wide the circle, of stumbling blocks that come from a single sin. In the book of Judges, we read how Micah made an idol for himself and his house, then hired a Levite to offer it sacrifices. The warriors of the tribe of Dan found out about this idol and stole it, and so the idol worship of a single man in a single household became the sin of an entire city and tribe. This is how sin usually works by using enticements and stumbling blocks. A sinful thought models an invisible idol of sin; an impure desire then carries it into the soul; a sinful action then carries it out and makes it visible. The carefully hidden secret of sin is thereby stolen and carried about; the stumbling block is born, and sin spreads. The weak-willed are enticed by evil example. Others fall into the sin of judgment against their neighbor. And what is there to say about sins which—either by their nature or by the brazenness or exalted social status of the sinner—cannot be hidden? What a plentiful sowing; what an extraordinary harvest!

How sorrowful, and yet how terrifying, are the words of the Lord concerning such stumbling blocks: *Woe to the world because of offenses! For offenses must come, but woe to that man by whom the offense comes! It would be better for him if a millstone were hung around his neck, and he were thrown into the sea, than that he should offend one of these little ones.* O merciful Lord! Concerning sins and sinners you speak with such calm and such meekness: *I did not come to call the righteous, but sinners, to repentance.* But concerning stumbling blocks and those who lay them in the path of their brother you speak so sorrowfully, so terrifyingly!

I have understood, O Lord, that Thy judgments are righteousness. Truly, sin is deplorable and terrifying, but stumbling blocks are far worse. By the grace of God, I can stop my own sin and cleanse it by my repentance. But if I lay a stumbling block before my brother, and my sin spreads to others, I am no longer able either to stop it or cleanse it.

Let us fear, brothers, to cause our brothers to fall! Let our care in avoiding laying stumbling blocks help us in our care to avoid sinning. Even so, we must run away from sin not only because we fear to cause our brothers to stumble, but because we find sin odious, and because we love God. As the Psalmist confessed, *I have hated and loathed untruth, but Thy law have I loved.*

Let us equally be afraid of laying stumbling blocks and stumbling ourselves, for sin is no less a sin if we are caused to sin by others. For it can give rise to yet new stumbling blocks. Do not let the brood of vipers continue to reproduce. Seek instead to cut off the head of the snake—the sinful thoughts—by the victorious power of the blameless Lamb, the all-pure Christ. Amen.

20

On Heavenly Rewards (1826)

"Rejoice in that day and leap for joy! For indeed your reward is great in heaven." (Luke 6:23)

The Lord Jesus commands us to rejoice and leap for joy. He promises us a reward, a great reward, a heavenly reward. Will any of us receive this reward, which is doubtless a perfect reward? For the Judge who gives it is just, and so He will give a worthy reward, and He is good, so He will give a generous reward, and He is all-powerful, so He will accomplish His own promise in the fullness of His power. Will any of us enter into such joy, which is doubtless a blessed joy? For He who calls us to this joy is the Source of blessedness.

Rejoice in that day! What is this day, pre-determined for joy? Will it come for us? Will we live long enough to see it?

Let us delve more deeply into the words of Christ, to better understand this pre-determined day. *Blessed are you when men hate you, and when they exclude you, and revile you, and cast out your name as evil, for the Son of Man's sake. Rejoice in that day and leap for joy!*

Luke 6:23

Luke 6:22-23

Thus, the day on which Christians rejoice and leap for joy is the time when they are hated, exiled, and dishonored for the name of Christ. Now do you want to live to see this day, to delight in this joy? Or do you want it to pass you by, even before you see it? Do you now not want to taste this joy whose taste you do not know? One cannot condemn the person who answers, in this situation, with the words of Christ Himself: *If it is possible, let this cup pass from me*, this cup of hatred from men, of persecutions, of dishonor. However, one cannot help but praise the one who has enough courage to constantly add these words of Christ to the aforementioned phrase: *nevertheless, not as I will, but as Thou wilt*, O Heavenly Father!

Matthew 26:39

Matthew 26:39

Though we leave it to the all-wise and inscrutable judgments of God to choose those worthy of the difficult labor and exalted blessedness of suffering for Christ, we must not fail to pay attention to that word of Christ that is instructive for all in general. In order to complete ascetic labors, and to overcome suffering, we must glean the necessary strength and the encouraging hope given to us in the promise of heavenly reward: *for your reward is great in heaven.*

Matthew 5:12

There are some—likely not many—exalted souls who, in their heart's thoughts and desires, walk by and ignore not only earthly, but even heavenly rewards. They strive directly, purely, exclusively to please God and to unite themselves with Him in the union of love. *For what have I in heaven*, said the Psalmist, *and what have I desired upon the earth from Thee? My flesh and my heart have failed, O God of my heart, but Thou art my portion, O God, for ever.* In other words, I do not desire anything earthly. Nor do I seek anything in the heavens, other than the God of heaven. My flesh does not seek sensual pleasures or the love of created beings. Without envy, I concede the most cherished human fate to everyone who desires them. My fate is God. My heart wants to cease existing in all places where it does not find Him, and it wants to be reborn in all places where He can be found. My very flesh languishes

Psalm 52:25-26

from the sole desire to be satisfied *when Thy glory is revealed.* For many of you standing here, I don't know what to tell you about this state of certain righteous souls, except to offer you these words of the Lord, spoken about one of these exceptional spiritual states: *He who is able to accept it, let him accept it.* *Psalm 16:15*

Matthew 19:12

However, even if the desire for reward is not the quality of the perfect, God does not forbid man to think of the reward. He even uses the thought of the reward to encourage man to fulfill the commandments and acquire perfection. *Honor your father and your mother*—this is a commandment. And immediately after it, follows the reward to encourage its fulfillment: *that your days may be long upon the land which the Lord you God is giving you.* Here, on the other hand, is a requirement for those who want to be perfect: *If you want to be perfect, go, sell what you have and give to the poor.* And yet, after this exalted command, the Lord again offers a reward to encourage the listener: *and you will have treasure in heaven.* *Exodus 20:12*

Matthew 19:12

Rejoice in that day, when men hate you, and when they exclude you, and revile you, and cast out your name as evil, for the Son of Man's sake." This is a heavy requirement for a labor that requires extraordinary power of spirit and unwavering endurance. Therefore, the reward is also great, capable of inspiring and upholding extraordinary fortitude: *for, behold, your reward is great in heaven.* *Luke 6:22-23*

The Old Testament, as a preparation for the perfection of Christianity, speaks in a more open way primarily about earthly rewards. This is because the people to whom the law was given were only capable of contemplating the spiritual blessedness of heaven through images of earthly prosperity. The New Testament, as the revelation of the perfection of the heavenly kingdom in its spiritual power and exalted purity, usually promises heavenly rewards to its ascetics and sufferers. Not only does it disdain earthly rewards as unimportant, but sometimes even considers them hindrances to heavenly rewards. *They have their reward,* said the Lord concerning the hypocrites who act virtu- *Matthew 6:2, 5, 16* ously for the sake of human praise. In other words, they have received their reward on earth, from men, and so they will not receive it in heaven from God. The Old Testament caressed people with earthly goods, but the Gospel warns that earthly goods are a danger. Disdain of earthly prosperity is a pledge of heavenly blessedness. *What will it profit a man if he gains the whole world, and loses his own soul? He who loves his life will lose it, and he who hates his life in this world will keep it for eternal life.*

<small>Mark 8:36
John 12:25</small>

According to such logic, every person who hears these words has an opportunity to offer to himself (or maybe even answer) this question: am I a Christian or not? If you are a true Christian, then you are truly not tied with your soul to temporary benefits. You have no passionate attachments to earthly rewards. You encourage and comfort yourself only with the thoughts of heavenly and eternal rewards. However, if you forget the eternal and heavenly reward, coveting temporary avarice, honors, the comforts of living for your own pleasures—do not delude yourself. Such a disposition does not reveal your spirit to be truly Christian. Whoever is directed and inspired by the desire only of earthly reward is an earthly "Old-Testamenter," far from spiritual perfection and from the acquisition of heavenly treasure. Whoever does good deeds for the sake of temporary gain or human glory has not yet abandoned the domain of paganism. Such a person makes idols out of his virtues, to be sold or to be presented as a spectacle for the praise of others. He will receive his reward from other people, and therefore the heavens and God Himself are no longer necessary for him.

Perhaps some will say that what I say is too strict, for it declares all to be under sin. For is it not natural, they will say, for man to seek the best in this life, just like a fish seeks out the deepest places? Let it be known to such people that I do not declare them to be prisoners of sin; rather it is the judgment of the word of Christ, and laziness to emulate this word—these declare you to be under sin. It may be natural to desire the best things in life; however, it does not accord with reason to seek these good things so much that we forget and lose the far better heavenly rewards. And if you wish to limit yourself by what is natural, then be aware, lest you lose by such limitation that which belongs to the realm of grace, which is far greater than nature. While you bulwark yourself with your so-called natural rights, are you not rejecting the following conditions of the law of grace: *Let your conduct be without covetousness; be content with such things as you have. Be kindly affectionate to one another with brotherly love, in honor giving preference to one another. Make no provision for the flesh, to fulfill its lusts.*

Hebrews 13:5
Romans 12:10
Romans 13:10

But what can we say about what is absolutely essential in the natural order of things? Should we seek earthly good things that are necessary for survival (keeping in mind that we do not call "necessary" that which is required by those who do not control their desires or rein in their passions)? When a hired worker desires to be paid enough to feed himself not only for the days of his work but also for the days of his rest, I do not argue that a desire for such a "reward" is natural. However, when a rich man does not want to do anything if he will not profit by it two times, or if possible, three times over, what is natural in this? When a government worker wants his salary to increase every year, wants extra pay for extra work, and expects greater and greater rank and privileges, what is natural in this? Does human nature demand these things? Does pouring money, ranks, or decorations on a person's head lead him to perfection?

Would it not be better, on the contrary, for the natural state of man if people did not have such high regard for earthly rewards? They are always insufficient compared to the labor required for their acquisition. They always give less joy compared to the unpleasantness of the seeking, the competition, the self-imposed deprivations of the one striving to receive them. How can they compare with heavenly rewards, which are always great, which give complete joy that cannot be taken away? If every person kept "the great reward in heaven" always before his eyes—and do not doubt that everyone can do so at all times—then, content with its expectation, no one would so passionately seek earthly rewards and temporary consolations. Every seller would be less concerned with gain. Every judge would more willingly prefer truth without bribes to the dishonorable gain of false judgment. The one who must serve society would zealously prefer the good of the many to his own personal gain. He would not swear off service to the common good, even if his service was not appreciated as it should be. He who is placed in subordination and obedience would more willingly forget his own will and would suffer less under the yoke of his master's severity. The slave would more zealously and joyfully work for his ungenerous master. In short, every person's renunciation of selfishness, upheld by the thought of heavenly reward, would constantly increase the treasure-house of humanity's common good, as well as the inner treasury of virtue found in every person's heart.

O Lord, generous in Thy promises and faithful in their fulfillment, confirm in us through fruitful remembrance and expectation this "great reward in heaven." May earthly rewards not allure us, and may no temporary sorrow or loss overwhelm us. Amen.

21

On Our Citizenship in Heaven (1833)

> *"For our citizenship is in heaven, from which we also eagerly wait for the Savior, the Lord Jesus Christ, who will transform our lowly body that it may be conformed to His glorious body, according to the working by which He is able even to subdue all things to Himself." (Philippians 3:20-21)*

It may be that our lives on this earth are sometimes pleasant. However, I hope no one will argue that our life in the heavens will be incomparably more pleasant, if only we can get there.

Therefore, is it not worth our time to pay attention to the Apostle's news concerning the life in the heavens—that it truly will come, and that it is something that belongs to us? For "our citizenship is in heaven."

This apostolic announcement of our heavenly citizenship may seem strange to an earthly mindset. It might protest: the birds of the sky do not live in heaven, even though they can separate themselves from the earth much easier than we do. Our life stands here on the earth, as on a foundation. It is nourished with earthly food. It wears earthly clothing. It finds shelter in an earthly home. How can you then say that our citizenship is in heaven? It would be a different thing if you said that our citizenship *will be* in heaven.

You justify me, brothers, in that I will not agree to correct or even weaken the words of the Apostle for the sake of those who don't understand. I stand firmly in the apostolic conviction that our citizenship is in heaven. To make this truth understandable and perceptible, I must contrast and compare the two lives—the temporary and the eternal, the earthly and the spiritual.

If you were to ask the citizen of a city during his travels in a field or through a village about his place of residence, he would doubtless not say, "I live on this road or here in this village inn." No, he would say that he lives in the city, where he has a house and a family, even if he was very far from that home at the time of questioning. And this is fair, for we do not live there, where we wander by accident or where we spend the night during a journey. We live where we have a permanent home. Apply the same reasoning to the words of the Apostle, and you will easily understand his words, though they may seem strange at first glance. St. Paul described this earthly life as only a journey. The world is no more than a wayside inn. Just as a wanderer anticipates coming home, and is, as it were, already there in his thoughts, even though he is still on the road, so also the heart of the Apostle, during his earthly wanderings, was already there where his treasure is, where God lives in light, where Christ rules in glory, where the saints live their true and eternal life. Thus did he reason and feel, and these same thoughts and emotions he assumed to exist in all Christians, since we all share the same faith and are the same heirs of eternal life. Therefore, he spoke not only for himself, but for all of us, when he said with conviction, *Our citizenship is in heaven.*

Philippians 3:20

Just as the temporary life is a barely noticeable instant when compared to eternity, so also the earthly (or sensual) life hardly deserves to be even called a life when compared to the spiritual life. As the holy Apostle declares our heavenly citizenship, he also sorrowfully and angrily rejects the physical or sensual life that predominates in certain people:

For many walk, of whom I have told you often, and now tell you even weeping, that they are the enemies of the cross of Christ: whose end is destruction, whose god is their belly, and whose glory is their shame—who set their mind on earthly things. — *Philippians 3:18-19*

Even a non-spiritual person will be upset if someone tells him that he lives only by his stomach. This is because even people who do not have a spiritual mindset still consider a gluttonous life to be odious. But consider this. If it is natural that every worshiper is much lower than the object of his adoration (his divinity, so to speak), then consider how deplorable are those people whose god is their belly, who offer sacrifices of time and life, body and soul, gifts of nature and gifts of earthly gain, all to the idol of sensual pleasures! If this is a life, it is no more than a cattle-life. There is no spark of a human life here, to say nothing of a Christian life!

What sort of life, then, is a life that we would not be ashamed to call our life? The life of the heart? Or the life of the mind? To this I answer concerning the life of the heart. If it is not exalted by special means, then it is very close to a sensual life, and so is easily cast down into the same abyss of deplorability that we have already described. Alternately, it is very easy to slip into the life of a beast who finds pleasure in tearing apart others. As for the life of the mind, I will begin by saying that only with difficulty, with the select few, does it rise to a certain height. Earthly reasoning still hangs over the same abyss of sensuality, and human nature has no strength to hold itself back from the edge.

Why does the Apostle place those *who set their minds on earthly things* on the same level as those *whose god is their belly*, that is, — *Philippians 3:19*
to those who, having abandoned themselves to sensuality, believe their glory to lie in shameful deeds, *whose end is destruction?* — *Philippians 3:19*
I ask again, what sort of a life can we call our own without exposing ourselves to shame or danger? Only this life—the life of the spirit, which *put[s] to death your members which are on the earth*

(i.e. all sensual desires and passions), by the power of the cross of Christ, that is, through submission to His commandments, and through emulation of His example. This is the life that brings *every thought into captivity to the obedience of Christ*, and that gives pure light to see the truth and power to unshakably stand in that truth. This is the life by which *Christ may dwell in your hearts through faith*, through love leading you to inner peace, to eternal blessedness. This is not an earthly life, for it kills the earthly. It is not earthly, because it is born of heavenly and divine seed. It is the heavenly life, because though it is sowed on earth, it grows in heaven, and even higher than the heavens. It is heavenly even before the end of the visible earthly life, because to us is declared *that eternal life which was with the Father and was manifested to us— that which we have seen and heard we declare to you, that you also may have fellowship with us; and truly our fellowship is with the Father and with His Son Jesus Christ*. This life is *the communion of the Holy Spirit"* with all of us. And this communion, without a doubt, is heavenly and surpassing the heavenly.

O Christians, let us come to know, let us truly feel the dignity of Christianity. Let us believe the exhortation of the Apostle. Let us come to understand this exhortation and find joy in it, *for our citizenship is in heaven*. And if we are still afraid of the vagaries of this temporary life, if we are still worried about the needs of our physical life, if we are still disturbed by temptations of the flesh, let us raise our gaze from the dark and mutable earth to the bright and immoveable heavens, *from which we also eagerly wait for the Savior, the Lord Jesus Christ*, who will finally end all vicissitudes of time, all needs of the body, and all temptations of the flesh, when He will *transform our lowly body that it may be conformed to His glorious body*, a process that He began for us by giving us hope through His Transfiguration, Resurrection, and Ascension.

SERMON 20: ON OUR CITIZENSHIP IN HEAVEN

Our citizenship is in heaven! In this apostolic utterance, I give you, children of the Church Militant, a weapon against many who battle you on this earth. *Philippians 3:20*

Does sorrow burden you over the heath of your beloved? Say to yourself, *Our citizenship is in heaven.* Surely it would not be wise to weaken yourself along the road with sorrow for those who have gone ahead of us. It would be better to focus our strength and attention to choose the right road to get to our common home. *Philippians 3:20*

Are you tempted by love for earthly things and a desire for monetary gain? Say to yourself, *Our citizenship is in heaven,* and here on earth we are only wanderers. A traveler should never burden himself too much along the road. It would be strange to stay on the side of the road, to build for yourself a magnificent house in the middle of a wilderness.

Are you subjected to ridicule? Have you lost your property, honor, reward? Tell yourself, *Our citizenship is in heaven.* There are our treasures which cannot be stolen, our imperishable crowns, our eternal rewards. We should not care overmuch if someone takes away our pennies along the road. Let us worry more about how to preserve our priceless inheritance in the home of our heavenly Father.

Thus, armed with this thought of the heavenly, this faith in the heavenly, this love for the heavenly, this hope for the heavenly, rise up above the earthly and above the nether parts of the earth, O you who were born on the earth. Labor without ceasing, and by grace heaven will reveal itself within you, and in the end, you will be in heaven with eternal glory. Amen.

After the Ascension of the Lord into heaven, the Apostles stood in place with their gazes fixed upward, as though they had nothing else left to do on this earth. When the Mother of God hid from this earth, invisibly ascending by the path of her Son into His divine glory, they had even less left on this earth. One doesn't want to look down to the earth when one sees that everything good, holy, divine, having shone in a moment like lightning, disappears equally quickly like lightning.

I would even be ready to sorrow today, but the Church tells us to rejoice. And this is doubtless because as it leads us to the edge of all that is earthly, it also leads us to the very threshold of heaven, revealing before our eyes the ladder to the heavens, by which not so long ago the living Ladder of Divinity had ascended. The Church wants us to enter there with a purified mind before becoming worthy of entering with a resurrected spirit and glorified body. It wants us to come to know the joyful truth, through an indubitable contemplation, of the apostolic words: *Our citizenship is in heaven, from which we also eagerly wait for the Savior, the Lord Jesus Christ, who will transform our lowly body that it may be conformed to His glorious body.*

Philippians 3:20

Lightning Source UK Ltd.
Milton Keynes UK
UKHW011320090720
366275UK00002B/731

9 781735 011608